**Oxford Reading Tree**

Planning your Literacy Hour
Trunk Stories Stages 1–9

Thelma Page

OXFORD
UNIVERSITY PRESS

OXFORD
UNIVERSITY PRESS

Great Clarendon Street, Oxford OX2 6DP

Oxford University Press is a department of the University of Oxford.
It furthers the University's objective of excellence in research,
scholarship, and education by publishing worldwide in

Oxford   New York
Athens   Auckland   Bangkok   Bogotá   Buenos Aires   Calcutta
Cape Town   Chennai   Dar es Salaam   Delhi   Florence   Hong Kong
Istanbul   Karachi   Kuala Lumpur   Madrid   Melbourne   Mexico City
Mumbai   Nairobi   Paris   São Paulo   Singapore   Taipei   Tokyo
Toronto   Warsaw

and associated companies in Berlin   Ibadan

Oxford is a registered trade mark of Oxford University Press in the UK
and in certain other countries

© Oxford University Press 1999
First published 1999

ISBN 0 19 919545 3

Cover illustration by Alex Brychta

Printed in the UK by Athenæum Press Ltd

Contents

Introduction 12

Year R
Stage 1 Stories without words

At School 14

Word work:	**W2** hearing and identifying initial sounds in words
Sentence work:	**S4** to use a capital letter for the start of own name
Text work:	**T1** to understand and use the terms *cover* and *title*
	T12 to write sentences to match pictures or sequences of pictures

The Lost Teddy 16

Word work:	**W2** hearing and identifying initial sounds in words
	W5 to read on sight a range of familiar words, e.g. children's names
Sentence work:	**S4** to use a capital letter for the start of own name
Text work:	**T1** to understand the use of the terms *beginning* and *end*
	T1 that words can be written down to be read again

The Street Fair 18

Word work:	**W1** to understand and be able to rhyme
	W4 discriminating 'onsets' from 'rimes' in spelling
	W5 to read on sight high frequency words for Year R from Appendix List 1
Sentence work:	**S3** that words are ordered left to right and need to be read that way
Text work :	**T1** to recognize words in a variety of settings, e.g. notices
	T7 to use knowledge of familiar texts to retell to others, recounting the main points in the correct sequence

Year R
Stage 1 First Words

Who Is It? 20

Word work:	**W2** writing *ch* and *sh* in response to each sound
	W6 to read on sight high frequency words for Year R Appendix List 1
Sentence work:	**S3** that words are ordered left to right and need to be read that way
Text work:	**T1** to understand the use of the term *page*
	T11 to understand how writing is formed, directionally, one word at a time

Six in a Bed 22

Word work:	**W3** understanding alphabetical order
	W6 to read on sight high frequency words for Year R Appendix List 1
	W7 to read on sight words from texts of appropriate difficulty
Sentence work:	**S3** that words are ordered left to right and need to be read that way
Text work:	**T1** to understand and use the terms *word*, *title*, and *page*
	T11 to understand that writing is constant, i.e. will always 'say' the same thing

Fun at the Beach 24

Word work:	**W3** sounding and naming letters in lower and upper case
	W2 hearing and identifying initial sounds in words
Sentence work:	**S1** to expect written text to make sense and check for sense if it does not
Text work:	**T1** to understand and use the term *letter*
	T11 to distinguish between writing and drawing in books

Year R
Stage 2 Stories and Stage 2 Wrens

The Toys' Party and *Good Old Mum* 26

Word work:	**W2** identifying and writing initial phonemes in CVC words	
	W7 to read on sight the words from texts of appropriate difficulty	
Sentence work:	**S1** to expect written text to make sense and check for sense if it does not	
Text work:	**T6** to reread a familiar text	
	T1 to track the text in the right order	
	T8 to locate and read significant parts of the text	
	T15 to use writing to communicate in a variety of ways	

New Trainers and *Fancy Dress* 28

Word work:	**W3** understanding alphabetical order
	W2 identifying and writing initial and dominant phonemes in spoken words
Sentence work:	**S1** to expect written text to make sense and check for sense if it does not
Text work:	**T9** to be aware of story structures
	T1 to track the text in the right order
	T11 to understand that writing remains constant

A New Dog and *The Pet Shop* 30

Word work:	**W4** identifying alliteration in known and new and invented words
	W1 extending rhyming patterns by analogy, generating new and invented words
Sentence work:	**S2** to use awareness of grammar of a sentence to predict words
Text work:	**T12** to experiment with writing in a variety of situations; to write sentences to match sequences of pictures
	T1 to track the text, pointing and making one to one correspondence between written and spoken text

What a Bad Dog! and *Push!* 32

Word work:	**W4** discriminating 'onsets' from 'rimes' in spelling
	W7 to read on sight words from texts of appropriate difficulty
	W14 to write letters using the correct sequence of movements
Sentence work:	**S2** to use awareness of grammar of a sentence to predict words
Text work:	**T8** to locate and read significant parts of the text
	T14 to use experience of stories as a basis for writing through substitution

The Go-Kart and *The Headache* 34

Word work:	**W6** to read on sight high frequency words from Year R list
	W2 identifying and writing initial and dominant phonemes in spoken words
Sentence work:	**S3** that words are ordered left to right and need to be read that way
Text work:	**T12** to write sentences to match pictures
	T2 to use a variety of cues when reading

The Dream and *At the Park* 36

Word work:	**W9** to recognize the critical features of words, e.g. shape
	W7 to read on sight words from texts of appropriate difficulty
Sentence work:	**S3** that words are ordered left to right and need to be read that way
Text work:	**T14** to use experience of stories as a basis for independent writing

Year 1 Term 1
Stage 3

On the Sand 38

    Word work: **W1** to practise and secure the ability to rhyme, and to relate this to spelling patterns

                     W9 to read on sight high frequency words from Appendix List 1

                     W3 to practise and secure the ability to hear initial and final phonemes in CVC words

    Sentence work: **S1** to expect written text to make sense and check for sense if it does not

    Text work: **T5** to describe story settings and relate to own experiences

                     T9 to write about events in personal experience linked to incidents from stories

The Dolphin Pool 40

    Word work: **W2** to practise and secure alphabetic knowledge

                     W3 to practise and secure the ability to hear initial and final phonemes in CVC words

    Sentence work: **S4** to write simple sentences, reread, recognizing whether they make sense

    Text work: **T4** to read independently, making correspondence between words said and read

                     T8 through shared writing to apply phonological, graphic knowledge, and sight vocabulary to spell words correctly

Nobody Wanted to Play 42

    Word work: **W10** to recognize critical features of words, e.g. words within words

                     W12 new words from reading and from shared experiences

                     W2 to practise and secure alphabetical order

    Sentence work: **S7** that a line of writing is not necessarily a sentence

    Text work: **T15** to make simple lists

                     T10 to use patterned stories as a model for writing

                     T2 to use phonological, contextual, grammatical, and graphic knowledge to predict and check the meaning of words

A Cat in the Tree 44

    Word work: **W6** to represent in writing the three phonemes in CVC words

    Sentence work: **S5** to recognize full stops and capital letters and name them correctly

    Text work: **T13** to read and follow simple instructions

                     T16 to write and draw simple instructions

The Rope Swing 46

    Word work: **W10** to recognize common features of words, e.g. common spelling patterns

                     W7 to read on sight high frequency words specific to graded books

    Sentence work: **S8** to begin to use full stops to demarcate sentences

    Text work: **T15** to use simple lists for reminding

                     T3 to notice the difference between spoken and written forms through retelling stories

By the Stream 48

    Word work: **W10** to recognize the critical features of words, e.g. length

                     W2 to secure alphabetic knowledge

                     W14 to form lower case letters correctly

    Sentence work: **S9** to use a capital letter for 'I' and for the start of a sentence

    Text work: **T9** to write about events in personal experience linked to incidents from stories

                     T7 to re-enact stories through role play

Year 1 Term 2
Stage 4

1: House for Sale 50
Word work: **W9** spell common words from Appendix List 1

W2 to investigate, read, and spell words ending in *ff, ll, ss, ck, ng*

Sentence work: **S3** predict words from preceding words

S5 to continue demarcating sentences in writing, ending with a full stop

Text work: **T15** build simple profiles of characters

T9 to become aware of character and dialogue

T16 to use some of the elements of known stories to structure own writing

2: The New House 52
Word work: **W10** make collections of words related to particular topics

Sentence work: **S7** use capital letters for names

Text work: **T14** represent outlines of story plots

T25 to assemble information from own experience

T2 to use phonological, contextual, grammatical, and graphic knowledge to work out new words

3: Come In! 54
Word work: **W6** read on sight high frequency words from Appendix List 1

W8 to investigate and learn spellings of words with s for plurals

Sentence work: **S1** expect text to make sense and to check for sense if it does not

S3 to predict words from preceding words in sentences

Text work: **T4** retell stories, giving main points in sequence

T9 to become aware of character an dialogue

4: The Secret Room 56
Word work: **W7** recognize critical features of words, e.g. length

W3 discriminate, read, and spell words with initial consonant clusters

Sentence work: **S3** predict words from preceding words

S5 to continue demarcating sentences in writing

Text work: **T14** present outlines of story plots using arrows

T16 to use some of the elements of known writing to structure own writing

5: The Play 58
Word work: **W3** discriminate, read, and spell words with initial consonant clusters

Sentence work: **S6** use the term sentence appropriately

Text work: **T16** use elements of known stories to structure own writing

T12 through shared writing to apply phonological, graphic knowledge, and sight vocabulary to spell words correctly

6: The Storm 60
Word work: **W2** investigate words ending in *ff, ll, ss, ck, ng*

W3 to discriminate, read, and spell words with initial consonant clusters

W11 handwriting; ensuring correct letter orientation, formation, and proportion

Sentence work: **S7** use capital letters for names

Text work: **T7** discuss reasons for, and causes of, incidents in stories

T16 to use some of the elements of known stories to structure own writing

Year 1 Term 3
Stage 5

1: The Magic Key 62

    Word work: **W5** recognize words by common spelling patterns

                      W1 to segment words into phonemes for spelling

    Sentence work: **S1** expect text to make sense and check for sense if it does not

                      S2 to use awareness of grammar to predict text

    Text work: **T13** write about significant incidents from known stories

                      T12 to apply phonological, graphic knowledge, and sight vocabulary to spell words accurately

2: Pirate Adventure 64

    Word work: **W9** to know the terms *vowel* and *consonant*

                      W1 to segment words into phonemes for spelling

    Sentence work: **S6** reinforce knowledge of the term *sentence*

                      S7 to add question marks to questions

    Text work: **T18** use words like *first, then, next*

                      T5 to retell stories; to pick out significant incidents

3: The Dragon Tree 66

    Word work: **W1** spelling patterns for long vowel phoneme ee and *ai*

    Sentence work: **S4** predict words from previous text, grouping a range of words that might 'fit'

    Text work: **T13** to write about significant incidents from stories

                      T21 to use labelled diagrams to show 'What we know about ...'

4: Gran 68

    Word work: **W6** investigate and learn spelling of verbs with *ed* and *ing*

                      W1 the common spelling patterns for long *oo* phoneme

    Sentence work: **S5** other common uses of capitalization

                      S7 to add question marks to questions

    Text work: **T7** use title, cover, etc. and 'blurbs' to predict content of stories

                      T12 to apply phonological, graphic knowledge, and sight vocabulary to spell words accurately

5: Castle Adventure 70

    Word work: **W4** read on sight common words (colours) from Appendix List 1

                      W1 to segment words into phonemes for spelling

                      W8 to collect words linked to a particular topic

    Sentence work: **S7** add question marks to questions

    Text work: **T16** compose carefully selected sentences

                      T21 to use captions for pictures to show 'What we know about ...'

6: Village in the Snow 72

    Word work: **W1** common spelling patterns for *oa* as in *boat*, *ie* as in *lie*

                      W1 the common spelling patterns for each long vowel phoneme

    Sentence work: **S2** predict text from the grammar

                      S6 through reading and writing to reinforce knowledge of the term *sentence*

                      S3 to read familiar texts aloud with pace and expression

    Text work: **T5** retell stories, giving main points in sequence

                      T12 to apply phonological, graphic knowledge, and sight vocabulary to spell words accurately

Year 2 Term 1
Stage 6

In the Garden 74

Word work: **W1** to secure identification, spelling, and reading of long vowel digraphs in simple words

Sentence work: **S1** to use awareness of grammar to decipher new or unfamiliar words

    S4 to reread their own writing for sense and punctuation

Text work: **T4** to understand time and sequential relationships in stories

    T10 to use story structure to write about own experience in similar form

Kipper and the Giant 76

Word work: **W3** the common spelling patterns for the vowel phonemes *oo* (as in *good*) *ar*, *oy*, *ow*

Sentence work: **S2** to find examples of words and phrases that link sentences

    S3 to recognize and take account of commas and exclamation marks when reading aloud

Text work: **T5** to identify and discuss reasons for events in stories, linked to plot

    T9 to apply phonological, graphic knowledge, and sight vocabulary to spell words accurately

The Outing 78

Word work: **W4** to investigate and classify words with the same sounds but different spellings

Sentence work: **S3** to recognize and take account of commas and exclamation marks in reading aloud

Text work: **T10** to use story structure to write about own experience in same/similar form

    T3 to be aware of the difference between spoken and written language

Land of the Dinosaurs 80

Word work: **W7** to use word endings (*s*, *ed*, *ing*) to support their reading and spelling

Sentence work: **S4** to reread own writing for sense and punctuation

Text work: **T11** to use language of time to structure a sequence of events

    T9 to apply phonological, graphic knowledge, and sight vocabulary to spell words accurately

Robin Hood 82

Word work: **W11** to practise handwriting patterns

    W12 to begin using and practising the four basic handwriting joins

    W5 to read and spell 30 more words from Appendix List 1

Sentence work: **S5** to revise knowledge about other uses of capitalisation and begin to use in own writing

    S3 to recognize and take account of commas and exclamation marks when reading aloud

Text work: **T15** to write simple instructions

    T18 to use appropriate register when writing instructions

The Treasure Chest 84

Word work: **W8** to secure understanding and use of the terms *vowel* and *consonant*

    W6 to read on sight high frequency words likely to occur in graded texts

Sentence work: **S6** to use simple organizatonal devices to indicate sequences and relationships

    S4 to reread own writing for sense and punctuation

Text work: **T18** to use appropriate register in writing instructions

    T12 to use simple poetry structures and to substitute own ideas

Year 2 Term 2
Stage 7

Red Planet 86

Word work:	**W2** the common spelling patterns for the vowel phonemes *air, or, er*
Sentence work:	**S4** to be aware for the need for grammatical agreement in speech and writing, matching verbs to nouns and pronouns correctly
Text work:	**T3** to discuss and compare story themes
	T13 to use story settings from reading, write a different story in the same setting

Lost in the Jungle 88

Word work:	**W4** to split familiar oral and written compound words into their component parts
	W2 to segment words into phonemes for spelling
Sentence work:	**S5** to use verb tenses with increasing accuracy in speaking and writing and to use the past tense consistently for narration
Text work:	**T5** to discuss story settings; to compare differences; to locate key words and phrases in text
	T13 to use story settings from reading to write a different story in the same setting

The Broken Roof 90

Word work:	**W5** to discriminate orally, syllables in multi-syllabic words using children's names
	W2 to segment words into phonemes for spelling
Sentence work:	**S6** to identify speech marks in reading, understand their purpose, use the term correctly
Text work:	**T6** to identify and describe characters, expressing own views
	T14 to write character profiles using key words or phrases that describe or are spoken by characters in the text

The Lost Key 92

Word work:	**W8** to spell words with common prefixes e.g. *un, dis* to indicate the negative
Sentence work:	**S7** to investigate and recognise a range of ways of presenting texts, e.g. speech bubbles
	S6 to identify speech marks in reading, understand their purpose, use the term correctly
Text work:	**T13** to use story settings from reading, e.g. write a different story in the same setting

The Motorway 94

Word work:	**W11** the use of antonyms: collect, discuss differences of meaning and their spelling
	W2 to segment words into phonemes for spelling
	W10 new words linked to particular topics
Sentence work:	**S8** to use commas to separate items in a list
Text work:	**T16** to use dictionaries to locate words by using the initial letter
	T3 to discuss and compare story themes
	T14 to write character profiles using key words or phrases that describe or are spoken by characters in the text

The Bully 96

Word work:	**W14** to use and practise the four basic handwriting joins
	W3 to read and spell words containing the digraphs *wh, ph, ch* (as in *Christopher*)
	W7 to read on sight high frequency words likely to occur in graded texts
Sentence work:	**S9** to secure the use of simple sentences in own writing
Text work:	**T14** to write character profiles, e.g. simple posters using key words or phrases that describe or are spoken by characters in the text

Year 2 Term 3
Stage 8

The Kidnappers 98

Word work: **W10** to use synonyms and other alternative words/phrases that express same or similar meanings

Sentence work: **S6** to turn statements into questions using a range of *wh* question words and to use question marks

S1 to read the text aloud with intonation and expression

Text work: **T13** to understand the distinction between fact and fiction; to use the terms *fact* and *fiction* appropriately

Viking Adventure 100

Word work: **W2** to reinforce work on discriminating syllables in reading and spelling from previous terms

Sentence work: **S3** to use standard forms of verbs in writing and to use the past tense consistently for narration

Text work: **T11** to invent language puzzles derived from reading

T4 to compare books by the same author

The Rainbow Machine 102

Word work: **W6** to investigate words that have the same spelling pattern but different sounds

W1 to secure phonemic spelling from previous five terms

Sentence work: **S5** to write in clear sentences using capital letters and full stops accurately

Text work: **T6** to read and respond imaginatively to humorous stories

T12 to write simple evaluations of books read and discussed giving reasons

The Flying Carpet 104

Word work: **W7** to spell words with the suffix *ly*

W1 to secure phonemic spelling from previous five terms

Sentence work: **S2** the need for grammatical agreement, matching verbs to nouns and pronouns; using simple gender forms correctly

Text work: **T2** to use contextual knowledge to work out, predict, and check the meanings of unfamiliar words and to make sense of what they read

T12 to write simple evaluations of books read and discussed giving reasons

T13 to understand the distinction between *fact* and *fiction*

A Day in London 106

Word work: **W3** to discriminate, read, and spell the phonemes *ear* (hear) and *ea* (head)

Sentence work: **S7** to compare a variety of questions from texts

S6 to turn statements into questions, learning a range of *wh* words

Text work: **T10** to write sustained stories using their knowledge of story elements

T13 to understand the distinction between *fact* and *fiction*

Victorian Adventure 108

Word work: **W4** to secure spelling of high frequency words in Appendix List 1

W5 to read on sight high frequency words likely to occur in graded texts

Sentence work: **S4** to use commas in lists

Text work: **T4** to compare books by the same author

T15 to use contents and index to find way about text

T13 to understand the distinction between *fact* and *fiction*

Year 2 Term 3
Stage 9

Green Island 110

    Word work: **W7** to spell words with common suffixes e.g. *fully*

    Sentence work: **S6** to turn statements into questions learning a range of *wh* words to open questions

    Text work: **T11** to write their own riddles and language puzzles

        T10 to write sustained stories, using their knowledge of story elements

Storm Castle 112

    Word work: **W10** to use synonyms and other alternative words and phrases that express same or similar meanings

    Sentence work: **S3** to use standard forms of verbs in writing and to use the past tense consistently for narration

    Text work: **T11** to write tongue twisters and alliterative sentences

        T9 to apply phonological, graphic knowledge, and sight recognition to spell words accurately

Superdog 114

    Word work: **W6** to investigate words with the same spelling patterns but different sounds

    Sentence work: **S5** to write in clear sentences using capital letters and full stops accurately

        S1 to read aloud with intonation and expression

    Text work: **T12** to write simple evaluations of books read and discussed, giving reasons

        T3 to notice the difference between spoken and written forms

The Litter Queen 116

    Word work: **W2** to reinforce work on discriminating syllables in reading and spelling

        W1 to secure phonemic spelling from previous five terms

    Sentence work: **S2** the need for grammatical agreement, matching verbs to nouns and pronouns using simple gender forms correctly

    Text work: **T10** to write sustained stories, using knowledge of story elements

The Quest 118

    Word work: **W1** to secure phonemic spelling from previous five terms

        W4 to secure reading and spelling of all the high frequency words from Appendix List 1

        W5 to read on sight high frequency words likely to occur in graded texts

    Sentence work: **S4** to use commas in lists

    Text work: **T10** to write sustained stories, using their knowledge of story elements

Survival Adventure 120

    Word work: **W1** to secure phonemic spelling from previous five terms (*or, oor, aw, au*)

    Sentence work: **S2** the need for grammatical agreement; using simple gender forms correctly

    Text work: **T13** to understand the distinction between fact and fiction; to use the terms *fact* and *fiction* appropriately

        T15 to use contents and index to find way about text

INTRODUCTION

These weekly plans suggest ways to use the trunk Oxford Reading Tree story books in the Literacy Hour. The books used are listed on the contents page together with teaching objectives covering word, sentence and text work from The National Literacy Strategy Framework. At each stage the stories are supported by a range of materials, including playscripts, work sheets, sequencing cards, context cards, and games. These materials are used in the plans to support the Teaching Objectives for each week.

The Oxford Reading Tree stages are matched to the years and terms of the NLS Framework as follows:

Stages 1 and 2 : Year R

Stage 3 : Year 1 Term 1

Stage 4 : Year 1 Term 2

Stage 5 : Year 1 Term 3

Stage 6 : Year 2 Term 1

Stage 7 : Year 2 Term 2

Stages 8 and 9 : Year 2 Term 3

The Range

Oxford Reading Tree stories meet the requirements for stories with predictable structure in Year R; stories with familiar settings (Year 1 Term 1), stories with familiar and predictable language (Year 1 Term 2) and for stories about fantasy worlds (Year 1 Term 3). In Year 2 there are stories with familiar settings (Term 1), stories with predictable and patterned language (Term 2) and extended stories by the same author (Term 3). Fact Finders, Rhyme and Analogy First Story Rhymes, Story Rhymes and the Poetry books help to meet the remaining requirements for a wide range of texts.

Shared Reading and Writing

These suggestions use the same story for shared reading and writing for the whole week.

The exception is at Stage 2 where each trunk story is supported by one of the Stage 2 Wrens. The Wrens story repeats selected key words on each page, giving reinforcement to children as they build a sight vocabulary.

At Stages 1–4 the suggestions include the use of the extended stories and guided responses published as photocopy masters. The guided response questions have been written to introduce the vocabulary and to enable the children to predict the text as they answer the question. Further questions encourage children to talk about their own experiences in circumstances similar to those of the story.

At Stages 5–9 questions from Teacher's Guides 2 and 3 enable children to predict the text, discuss causes and effects, think about characters and encourage discussion of more general topics arising from the story. Page references for these questions are included in the notes.

Teachers will find the box of Context Cards available for Stages 1–5 very useful when focusing on the sequence of events in a story, the punctuation of a sentence, and when practising key words.

Sequencing Cards Photocopy Masters for Stages 1–4 enable the children to put pictures and sentences in order and to retell the story. There is a suggestion for a shared writing activity each week. This arises from the story and includes writing lists, rhymes and posters, and planning, retelling, or changing stories.

NB Some teachers at Year 2 and above find that setting aside one Literacy Hour each week for shared, guided, and independent writing enables children to write at greater length. In this case you could use the shared writing suggestion as a starting point and then work with one or two groups while the others all write independently.

Word Work

The focus of each week's word work usually arises from the text and is then developed to include a wide range of examples. Each week the word work suggestions include time for 'words or sounds of the week' so that children continually build upon their phonological knowledge and sight recognition of high frequency words.

Guided Group Tasks (reading or writing)

It is not expected that the book used by groups in guided reading will be the same as the shared text. However, the trunk stories are ideal for guided group work and therefore reading and writing activities based on the story and the general ability level of the children have been suggested. These suggestions will support teachers who choose to use that particular title with a group, having used a different title for shared reading, possibly a non-fiction or a poetry book.

The focus of guided reading sessions arises from the specific needs of the children. At the early stages this involves reinforcing the use of a variety of cues and strategies to read and make sense of new words. For more fluent readers the focus is likely to be upon vocabulary extension, comprehension, and a personal response to the text.

Independent Group Work

Worksheets based upon each trunk story used in the shared reading sessions have been designed to reinforce teaching objectives at text, sentence, and word level for the week. These are available as photocopy masters in Group Activity Sheets Books 1, 2, and 3. For children who finish quickly there is a suggestion for a further activity to extend the task.

Written work and games from Teacher's Guides 1, 2 and 3 are also suggested as independent group activities. These activities are either based directly upon the story or suggest activities for learning key words at that stage.

Other suggestions include: listening to the story tapes for Stages 1–4; using the CD-Rom Talking Stories for Stages 2 and 3; reading playscripts for Stages 4–9; using workbooks for all the stages and a choice of familiar stories.

The Rhyme and Analogy Alphabet frieze and Table Top mats are valuable when children are learning initial sounds and alphabetical order. Rhyme and Analogy Card Games enable children to practise the alphabet, initial sounds, and rhyming words.

Games Boxes at Stages 1–3, 4 and 5 and 6–9* provide games that practise and reinforce word, sentence, and text level objectives. They are intended to be played with an adult or a more able child initially. Once the children are familiar with the games they can be played independently.

Plenary

The plan shows suggestions for specific groups to explain their work or for a reinforcement activity.

Assessment

Guided reading and writing sessions provide the opportunity for continuous assessment of children's attainment. By praising achievements and setting targets, teachers give children feedback on their own progress. In addition the weekly plans suggest assessing the child's knowledge of high frequency words and key words at the end of Stages 2–9. Further suggestions for assessment are included in *Group Activity Sheets Books 1, 2,* and *3*. These sheets include word building activities to assess children's phonological awareness, high frequency and key word lists, and ways to use a text extract to assess a variety of teaching objectives.

*Games Box Stages 6–9 will be available January 2000.

Stage 1   At School   Year R

Shared reading and writing

Monday: Introduce the book by looking at the cover, the title, and the pictures. Decide what the book might be about. Read the extended story while looking at the pages. Use the questions suggested for each page to involve the children.

Tuesday: Retell the story or reread the extended story. Let the children talk about their own first day at nursery or at school.

Wednesday: Reread the story. Ask the children to notice names and find the people in the pictures (e.g. Miss Harvey, Mum, Caroline and Tony).

Thursday: Ask the children to read the title and retell the story page by page.

Friday: Shared writing: Prepare strips of paper to attach to each page. Ask the children to suggest what to write for each page. Read the children's story.

Word work

Initial sounds in words. Capital letters at the beginning of names.

Monday: Name objects in the pictures; listen for the initial sound of each one. Use the pictures to play 'I spy'.

Tuesday: Use objects and pictures. Practise hearing and identifying initial sound(s) of the week.

Wednesday: Capital letters for names: write names mentioned in the extended story on pieces of paper. Ask the children to identify people in the pictures. Attach a name to each one. Draw attention to the capital letter each time.

Thursday: Look at the bricks on pages 6 and 7. Identify each one by sound; think of a word that starts with each sound.

Friday: Practise this week's letter sounds.

Guided group tasks (reading or writing)

Reading: Ask the children to find the title and look at the cover. Read the title together. Read the extended story while the children look at the pages. Use the questions to help children explain what is happening in the story. Encourage children to retell the story.

Writing: Help the children to form letters correctly when writing their own names.

Independent activities

1: Listen to the story tape or use Stage 1 workbooks.

Group Activity Sheets Book 1: Use the notes on page 13 to introduce the following:

2: Word work (page 14) for hearing and identifying initial sounds in words.

3: Sentence work (page 15) to use capital letters for the start of names.

4: Text work (page 16) to understand and use the terms *cover* and *title*.

5: Games Box for Stages 1–3: Card game for matching names to characters, with an adult if possible. Or use 'Draw the face' game on Activity Sheet 1.2, explained on page 84 in *Teacher's Guide 1*.

Plenary

Use this time to allow children to explain their work to others. It is also an opportunity to reinforce teaching points as they arise and to add to the morning's word work.

Suggested Weekly Plan　　AT SCHOOL　　STAGE 1　　YEAR R

Day	Whole class – shared reading and writing	Whole class – phonics, spelling, vocabulary, grammar	Guided group tasks (reading or writing)	Guided group tasks (reading or writing)	Independent group tasks				Plenary
Mon	Read extended story and use suggested questions.	Find and name objects in the pictures. Talk about the sound they begin with.	**Group A** Guided reading. GAS Bk1 p14. (T)	**Group B** Story tape or workbooks. Guided reading or writing. (T)	**Group C** Writing names, GAS Bk1 p15. Practise writing name. (I)	**Group D** Covers and titles, GAS Bk1 p16.	**Group E** Games with character cards, Games Box 1–3.		**Group C** Show work. **Group D** Show work.
Tues	Retell or read extended story. Let children tell own experiences.	Practise hearing and identifying this week's letter sounds.	**Group B** As above (T)	**Group C** As above (T)	**Group D** As above (I)	**Group E** As above	**Group A** As above or key word game. (OA)		**Group E** Show work. **Group A** Explain games they played.
Wed	Reread the extended story. Ask children to find people named in the story in the illustrations.	Write names on paper and attach to picture using blu-tack. Talk about capital letters for names.	**Group C** As above (T)	**Group D** As above (T)	**Group E** As above (I)	**Group A** Word lotto Stage 4 or 5, Games Box 4–5.	**Group B** As above (OA)		**Group B** Explain their games. Reread names attached to book.
Thur	Let children read the title and retell the story page by page.	Look for letters on bricks in picture. Children suggest words beginning with those sounds.	**Group D** As Group A (T)	**Group E** As above (T)	**Group A** As above (I)	**Group B** As above	**Group C** As above (OA)		Play I-spy with objects in the room.
Fri	Ask children what to write as caption for each page. Teacher scribes.	Practise this week's letter sounds.	**Group E** As above (T)	**Group A** As above (T)	**Group B** As above (I)	**Group C** As above	**Group D** As above (OA)		Reread the shared story together.

Fitting in with the National Literacy Framework

Word work: W2 hearing and identifying initial sounds in words.

Sentence work: S4 to use a capital letter for the start of own name.

Text work: T1 to understand and use the terms cover and title; **T12** to write sentences to match pictures or sequences of pictures.

T = Teacher　　**I = Independent**　　**OA = Other adult**

These weekly plans are intended as exemplars only and teachers will want to exercise their own skill and judgement when planning for the Literacy Hour.

Stage 1　　　The Lost Teddy　　　Year R

Shared reading and writing

Monday: Introduce the book by looking at the cover, the title, and the pictures. Decide what the book might be about. Read the extended story while looking at the pages. Use the questions suggested for each page to involve the children.

Tuesday: Retell the story or reread the extended story. Let the children talk about times when they have lost something precious.

Wednesday: Introduce the terms *beginning* and *end*. Talk about what happened at the beginning and at the end of the story. Ask children to find the beginning and the end of the story.

Thursday: Shared writing: Ask the children what Kipper is thinking on each page. The teacher writes the thoughts on 'thought clouds' and attaches them to each page. Read the writing together.

Friday: Ask the children to retell the story in their own words. Read Kipper's thoughts together.

Word work

Initial sounds in words; capital letters at the beginning of names.

Monday: Write *Kipper*, *teddy*, and *Mum* several times each on pieces of card. Draw attention to the initial sound of each word. Children to find the right picture on the page and attach the name.

Tuesday: Practise reading the name cards. Practise hearing and identifying this week's letter sounds.

Wednesday: Read name cards for Kipper and Mum. Notice capital letters. Read children's names on cards or labels. Notice capital letters at the beginning of each.

Thursday: Use objects and pictures to practise hearing and identifying this week's letter sounds.

Friday: Practise this week's letter sounds.

Guided group tasks (reading or writing)

Reading: Ask the children to find the title and look at the cover. Read the title together. Ask children what is happening at the beginning of the story. Read the extended story as the children look at the right page of the book. What happens at the end?

Writing: Ask each child to draw his or her own favourite toy and write its name. Say the name of the toy clearly yourself and help the children to recognise the sounds in the name.

Independent activities

1: Listen to the story tape or use Stage 1 workbooks.

Group Activity Sheets Book 1: Use the notes on page 17 to introduce the following:

2: Word work (page 18) for hearing and identifying initial sounds in words.

3: Sentence work (page 19) to use a capital letter for the start of names.

4: Text work (page 20) to understand and use the terms *beginning* and *end*.

5: Games Box for Stages 1–3: Card game for matching names to characters, with an adult if possible. Or play 'Racing home' using Activity Sheet 1.3, explained on page 84 of *Teacher's Guide 1*.

Plenary

Use this time to allow children to explain their work to others. It is also an opportunity to reinforce teaching points as they arise and to add to the morning's word work.

Suggested Weekly Plan — THE LOST TEDDY — STAGE 1 — YEAR R

	Whole class – shared reading and writing.	Whole class – phonics, spelling, vocabulary, grammar.	Guided group tasks (reading or writing)	Guided group tasks (reading or writing)	Independent group tasks			Plenary
Mon	Look at the cover and the illustrations to predict what happens. Read the extended story.	Write *Kipper, teddy,* and *Mum* several times on cards. Children to find and attach them to pictures.	**Group A** Guided reading. GAS Bk1 p18.	**Group B** Story tape or workbooks. Guided reading or writing.	**Group C** Names have capital letters, GAS Bk1 p19. Write name.	**Group D** Beginning and ending, GAS Bk1 p20.	**Group E** 'Draw the face' game, TGI p84 AS 1.2.	**Groups A and C** Show and talk about their work.
Tues	Read the story and ask the questions suggested. Let children talk about own experiences.	Practise reading *Mum, Kipper, teddy.* Use objects or pictures to practise initial sound recognition.	**Group B** As above	**Group C** As above	**Group D** As above	**Group E** As above	**Group A** As above	**Groups E and D** Show and talk about their work.
Wed	Children retell the story, talk about what happened at the beginning and the end of the story.	Notice capital letters for *Kipper* and *Mum.* Read children's names on cards.	**Group C** As above	**Group D** As above	**Group E** As above	**Group A** Word lotto Stage 4 or 5, Games Box 4-5.	**Group B** As above	**Group B** Explain their game and show their work.
Thur	Look at the pictures and talk about what Kipper is thinking. Write thoughts on 'thought clouds'.	Practise initial sound recognition using objects or pictures.	**Group D** As group A	**Group E** As above	**Group A** As above	**Group B** As above	**Group C** As above	Read Kipper's thoughts. Find children's names on cards or on displays/drawers.
Fri	Children retell the story in own words, reading what Kipper is thinking.	Practise/revise this week's high frequency words or letter sounds.	**Group E** As above	**Group A** As above	**Group B** As above	**Group C** As above	**Group D** As above	Read what Mum said. Praise good work done this week.

T = Teacher   I = Independent   OA = Other adult

Fitting in with the National Literacy Framework

Word work: W2 hearing and identifying initial sounds in words; W5 to read on sight a range of familiar words, e.g. children's names.

Sentence work: S4 to use a capital letter for the start of own name.

Text work: T1 to understand and use the terms *beginning* and *end*; T1 that words can be written down to be read again.

These weekly plans are intended as exemplars only and teachers will want to exercise their own skill and judgement when planning for the Literacy Hour.

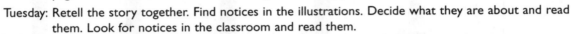

Stage 1   The Street Fair   Year R

Shared reading and writing

Monday: Introduce the book by looking at the cover, the title, and the pictures. Decide what the book might be about. Read the extended story while looking at the pages. Was this what the children thought would happen?

Tuesday: Retell the story together. Find notices in the illustrations. Decide what they are about and read them. Look for notices in the classroom and read them.

Wednesday: Retell the story asking the questions from the extended story. Ask the children about having their own faces painted.

Thursday: Encourage volunteers to tell the story to the class, turning the pages themselves.

Friday: Shared writing: Enlarge the four pictures for *The Street Fair* from Sequencing Cards from A4 to A3. Cut into four pictures. Ask children to make up a sentence to fit each. The teacher scribes.

Word work

Words that rhyme; recognizing 'and' in print.

Monday: Enlarge page 22 from *Group Activity Sheets Book 1*. Use the words and pictures to find pairs that rhyme. Ask children to draw mapping lines to join rhyming pairs.

Tuesday: Use words from the above page and show children how to change the onset to create more rhyming words, e.g. *man, van, can, ran, fan,* etc. The teacher writes the words under each other, so that children can see that only the first letter changes, and the rime stays the same in each list.

Wednesday: Find words in the notices and ask children to change the onset to create rhymes, e.g. *fun, bun, face, lace.*

Thursday: Use 'Handy and' activity, page 84 *Teacher's Guide 1*, to link children and read the names with 'and'.

Friday: Practise this week's letter sounds.

Guided group tasks (reading or writing)

Reading: Read the title together. Ask children what is happening at the beginning of the story. Read the extended story. What happens at the end? Find notices in the illustrations. How can you work out what they say?

Writing: Practise writing 'It is' sentences, ending each one with a name from the story or from the class. Emphasize starting at left-hand side of the page each time.

Independent activities

1: Listen to the story tape.

Group Activity Sheets Book 1: Use the notes on page 21 to introduce the following:

2: Word work (page 22) to understand and be able to rhyme.

3: Sentence work (page 23) so that words are ordered left to right.

4: Text work (page 24) to recognize words in notices.

5: Games Box for Stages 1–3: Key words game, with an adult if possible. Or use 'Fish and chips' Activity Sheet 1.4, explained on page 84 of *Teacher's Guide 1*.

Plenary

Use this time to allow children to explain their work to others. It is also an opportunity to reinforce teaching points as they arise and to add to the morning's word work.

Suggested Weekly Plan — THE STREET FAIR — STAGE 1 — YEAR R

	Whole class – shared reading and writing.	Whole class – phonics, spelling, vocabulary, grammar.	Guided group tasks (reading or writing)	Guided group tasks (reading or writing)	Independent group tasks			Plenary
Mon	Use the title and pictures to predict the story, then read extended story to see if predictions were right.	Talk about words that rhyme. Enlarge p22 from GAS Bkl. Match rhyming words with mapping lines.	**Group A** Guided reading. Order sequencing cards and write own sentences. (T)	**Group B** Story tape or workbooks. Guided reading or writing. (T)	**Group C** 'It is' sentences, GAS Bk1 p23. (I)	**Group D** Words in notices, GAS Bk1 p24. (I)	**Group E** Key words game, Games Box 1–3. (OA)	Find objects in the room to name and think of rhymes for them.
Tues	Retell the story together. Find and read all the notices in the pictures and classroom.	Separate onset and rime. Change onset to create rhyming words, e.g. *man, van, can, ran* etc.	**Group B** As above (T)	**Group C** As above (T)	**Group D** As above (I)	**Group E** As above (I)	**Group A** Key words game, Games Box 1–3. (OA)	**Groups D and E** Show and talk about their work.
Wed	Retell the story, asking questions from the extended story.	Find words in notices and ask children to suggest words that rhyme, e.g. *fun, face.*	**Group C** As above (T)	**Group D** As above (T)	**Group E** As above (I)	**Group A** Word lotto Stage 4 or 5, Games Box 4–5. (I)	**Group B** As above (OA)	**Group C** Read own sentences.
Thur	Let children volunteer to retell the story and turn the pages themselves.	Use name cards and 'and' as flashcards. Use the 'handy and' activity, TG1 p84.	**Group D** As group A (T)	**Group E** As above (T)	**Group A** As above (I)	**Group B** As above (I)	**Group C** As above (OA)	**Groups A and B** Show and talk about their work.
Fri	Enlarge and use the four sequencing cards for the story. Children put them in order.	Practise/revise this week's high frequency words or letter sounds.	**Group E** As above (T)	**Group A** As above (T)	**Group B** As above (I)	**Group C** As above (I)	**Group D** As above (OA)	Reread the class story. Read independent stories written earlier this week.

Fitting in with the National Literacy Framework

Word work: W1 to understand and be able to rhyme; **W4** discriminating 'onsets' from 'rimes' in speech and spelling; **W5** read on sight high frequency words for Year R from Appendix List 1.

Sentence work: S3 that words are ordered left to right and need to be read that way to make sense.

Text work: T1 to recognize words in a variety of settings, e.g. notices; **T7** to use knowledge of familiar texts to retell to others, recounting the main points in the correct sequence.

T = Teacher   **I = Independent**   **OA = Other adult**

These weekly plans are intended as exemplars only and teachers will want to exercise their own skill and judgement when planning for the Literacy Hour.

Stage I First Words   Who Is It?   Year R

Shared reading and writing

Monday: Introduce the book by looking at the cover, the title, and the pictures. Decide what the book might be about. Read the extended story while looking at the pages. Was this what the children thought would happen?

Tuesday: Retell the story or reread the extended story. Play a 'Who is it?' game by describing children without saying the name. Children say 'It is ...'.

Wednesday: Retell the story. On each page point to words as children read. Let one child turn the pages.

Thursday: Shared writing: Ask the children to suggest whole sentences for each page, e.g. 'Biff and Chip made shadows.' Attach extra paper to each page so that you can write the rest of the sentence. Read the new sentences.

Friday: Read the new sentences written yesterday. Ask children to point to the words as they read.

Word work

Recognize high frequency words: *and, it, is, a* and names from Stage I; introduce *sh* and *ch* phonemes.

Monday: Use 'and' to link names; use children's names and names from Stage I stories.

Tuesday: Practise reading *it, is, a, and* out of context. Order words to make sentences, e.g. 'It is Kipper.'

Wednesday: Collect *sh* words. Write them on a shadow shape.

Thursday: Collect *ch* words. Write them on an outline of Chip. (See *Teacher's Guide I* Character Sheet 4.)

Friday: Practise and revise this week's high frequency words and letter sounds.

Guided group tasks (reading or writing)

Reading: Read the title together. Read the extended story. Read the text. Ask children to find the page number on each page. Practise finding different page numbers.

Writing: Practise writing 'It is ... and ... ' sentences, using names from the story or from the class. Remind children to start at left-hand side of the page each time.

Independent activities

1: Listen to the story tape or use Stage I workbooks.

Group Activity Sheets Book I: Use the notes on page 25 to introduce the following:

2: Word work (page 26) to write *ch* and *sh* in response to each sound.

3: Sentence work (page 27) so that words are ordered left to right.

4: Text work (page 28) to understand and use the term *page*.

5: Rhyme and Analogy Card Games: Sort and match words and pictures with *sh* and *ch* sounds.

6: Trace and write own names then names from Stage I stories.

Plenary

Use this time to allow children to explain their work to others. It is also an opportunity to reinforce teaching points as they arise and to add to the morning's word work.

Suggested Weekly Plan — WHO IS IT? — STAGE 1 FIRST WORDS — YEAR R

	Whole class – shared reading and writing.	Whole class – phonics, spelling, vocabulary, grammar.	Guided group tasks (reading or writing)	Guided group tasks (reading or writing)	Independent group tasks			Plenary
Mon	Read the title, look at the pictures, and predict what is happening. Read the extended story.	Revise names on flashcards with 'and'. Make various combinations with three children holding the words.	**Group A** Guided reading. 'It is' sentences with 'and', GAS Bk1 p27. — T	**Group B** Story tape or workbooks. Guided reading or writing. — T	**Group C** Finding words from the book, GAS Bk1 p28. — I	**Group D** Handwriting; practise own name, then Biff, Chip, Kipper. — I	**Group E** Sort sh and ch from R& A cards, GAS Bk1 p26. — OA	**Group E** Explain how they sorted sh and ch cards. Suggest more words for each set.
Tues	Read the extended story and use the discussion questions.	Practise reading is, it, a, and out of context.	**Group B** As above — T	**Group C** As above — T	**Group D** As above — I	**Group E** As above — I	**Group A** As above — OA	**Group D** Explain how they looked for the shadows in the book and wrote the words.
Wed	Children read the story, pointing to words and turning pages.	Talk about shadow starting with sh; think of more sh words.	**Group C** As above — T	**Group D** As above — T	**Group E** As above — I	**Group A** Word lotto Stage 4 or 5, Games Box 4–5. — I	**Group B** As above — OA	Reread list of sh words. **Group C** Show sentences.
Thur	Children suggest sentences for each page, e.g. 'Biff and Chip made shadows.' Teacher scribes.	Talk about Chip starting with ch. Think of more ch words.	**Group D** As group A — T	**Group E** As above — T	**Group A** As above — I	**Group B** As above — I	**Group C** As above — OA	Reread new text written for the story. Add to ch list.
Fri	Read sentences written yesterday. Take turns to read, point to words.	Practise/revise this week's high frequency words or letter sounds.	**Group E** As above — T	**Group A** As above — T	**Group B** As above — I	**Group C** As above — I	**Group D** As above — OA	Think of words ending with sh, e.g. push, rush.

Fitting in with the National Literacy Framework

Word work: W2 writing sh and ch in response to each sound; **W6** to read on sight high frequency words for Year R from Appendix List 1.

Sentence work: S3 that words are ordered left to right and need to be read that way to make sense.

Text work: T1 to understand and use the term page; **T11** to understand how writing is formed directionally, a word at a time.

T = Teacher   **I = Independent**   **OA = Other adult**

These weekly plans are intended as exemplars only and teachers will want to exercise their own skill and judgement when planning for the Literacy Hour.

Stage 1 First Words   Six in a Bed   Year R

Shared reading and writing

Monday: Introduce the book by looking at the cover, the title, and the pictures. Ask the children if they can see any words they know already. Read the extended story. Point to the words in order while the children read the text.

Tuesday: Read the extended story and ask the questions suggested. Count the number of people in the bed on each page.

Wednesday: Shared writing: Ask the children how many are in the bed on each page. Write captions 'Two in the bed,' 'Three in the bed' etc … Read and attach the captions to the right pages.

Thursday: Children read text as teacher points to each word. Read the captions written yesterday together.

Friday: Ask the children to tell the story from memory in their own words. Take turns to read the original text, pointing at each word in turn and turning the pages.

Word work

Practise the alphabet in order; practise high frequency words.

Monday: Learn or practise the alphabet song or chant it together. Practise saying the letters in turn around the class, or pairs who know it well say alternate letters to the rest of the class.

Tuesday: Practise the alphabet as above. Use the Rhyme and Analogy Alphabet Frieze or Table Top Alphabet Cards as prompts.

Wednesday: Use flash cards to consolidate and practise Stage 1 key words and high frequency words from the list for Year R in Appendix List 1 of the NLS Framework.

Thursday: Practise the alphabet. Choose letters at random and ask children what comes next?

Friday: Practise this week's high frequency words or letter sounds.

Guided group tasks (reading or writing)

Reading: Ask the children to find the title of the book. Read the extended story. Read the text. Practise finding different page numbers. Reinforce understanding of the term 'word' by asking children to 'Find a word beginning with M' etc.

Writing: Practise writing letters with similar formation.

Independent activities

1: Listen to the story tape or use Stage 1 workbooks.

Group Activity Sheets Book 1: Use the notes on page 29 to introduce the following:

2: Word work (page 30) to understand alphabetical order.

3: Sentence work (page 31) so that words are ordered left to right.

4: Text work (page 32) to understand and use the terms *word*, *title*, and *page*.

5: Rhyme and Analogy Card Games: Sort and match complete alphabets using letter cards. Match a picture to each letter.

6: Have a variety of ABC books and picture dictionaries for children to choose from.

Plenary

Use this time to allow children to explain their work to others. It is also an opportunity to reinforce teaching points as they arise and to add to the morning's word work.

Suggested Weekly Plan — SIX IN A BED — STAGE I FIRST WORDS — YEAR R

	Whole class – shared reading and writing.	Whole class – phonics, spelling, vocabulary, grammar.	Guided group tasks (reading or writing)	Guided group tasks (reading or writing)	Independent group tasks			Plenary
Mon	Look at cover and pictures. Recognise and read familiar words. Read extended story.	Sing or say ABC rhyme. Practise saying alphabet in turn around the class, or in pairs taking turns.	**Group A** (most able) Guided reading. GAS Bk1 p31. — T	**Group B** GAS Bk1 p30. Guided reading or writing. — T	**Group C** Order alphabet using Rhyme and Analogy cards or letters. — I	**Group D** ABC books and dictionaries to read. Use CD-Rom dictionary. — I	**Group E** Word, page, and title, GAS Bk1 p32. — OA	Read simple ABC book together. **Group B** Show dot to dot ABC.
Tues	Read extended story and ask questions suggested.	Practice saying or singing alphabet, use table top mats or frieze to prompt.	**Group E** As above — T	**Group A** As above — T	**Group B** As above — I	**Group C** As above — I	**Group D** As above — OA	**Group C** Show favourite pages from A-Z books.
Wed	Write captions 'Two in a bed', 'Three in a bed' etc. to match to right pictures.	Use flash cards to consolidate Stage I/high frequency words.	**Group D** As above — T	**Group E** As above — T	**Group A** As above — I	**Group B** Word lotto Stage 4 or 5, Games Box 4–5. — I	**Group C** As above — OA	**Groups D and E** Show work. Practise high frequency words.
Thur	Children read text, pointing at words. Match and read new text written yesterday.	What comes next? Show magnetic letter at random. Children say what comes next in alphabet.	**Group C** As group A — T	**Group D** As above — T	**Group E** As above — I	**Group A** As above — I	**Group B** As above — OA	**Group A** Show favourite pages from A-Z books. Sing alphabet song.
Fri	Take turns to read text, turning pages and pointing to words.	Practise/revise his week's high frequency words or letter sounds.	**Group B** As above — T	**Group C** As above — T	**Group D** As above — I	**Group E** As above — I	**Group A** As above — OA	Play 'What comes next?' alphabet game as Thursday word work.

Fitting in with the National Literacy Framework

Word work: W3 understanding alphabetical order; **W6** to read on sight high frequency words for Year R from Appendix List 1; **W7** to read on sight words from texts of appropriate difficulty.

Sentence work: S3 that words are ordered left to right and need to be read that way to make sense.

Text work: T1 to understand and use the terms *word, title,* and *page;* **T11** to understand that writing remains constant, i.e. will always 'say' the same thing.

T = Teacher　　**I = Independent**　　**OA = Other adult**

These weekly plans are intended as exemplars only and teachers will want to exercise their own skill and judgement when planning for the Literacy Hour.

Stage I First Words   Fun at the Beach   Year R

Shared reading and writing

Monday: Introduce the book by looking at the cover, the title, and the pictures. Ask the children if they can see any words they know already. Read the extended story. Point to the words in order while the children read the text.

Tuesday: Read the extended story and ask the questions suggested. Ask the children to talk about their own experiences on a pier or in a hall of mirrors.

Wednesday: Ask the children to retell the story from memory. Read the text together. Read all the notices to the children.

Thursday: Shared writing: Children suggest the rest of sentence on each page, e.g. '… were on the pier.' Using extra strips of paper, the teacher writes down children's ideas and fixes the paper to the page.

Friday: Children take turns to read text. Read new captions together. Read the notices in classroom.

Word work

Revise alphabetical order. Match lower case letters to capitals. Revise initial sounds.

Monday: Use magnetic letters to put alphabet in order. Match capital letters in order underneath. Read both alphabets.

Tuesday: Use magnetic letters or letter cards and give one letter to each child. (If more than 26 children you need extra cards.) Show capital letters one at a time and ask the child with the matching lower case letter to claim it. Ask child which letter (sound and name if possible) he or she has collected.

Wednesday: Look at GRAND PIER on the cover. Use lower case magnetic letters to write it in lower case. Find more notices in the book. Use magnetic letters to change notices in lower case to all capitals.

Thursday: Use a collection of objects and pictures to revise initial sounds in words.

Friday: Practise this week's high frequency words and letter sounds.

Guided group tasks (reading or writing)

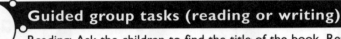

Reading: Ask the children to find the title of the book. Read the extended story. Read the text. Find notices in the book. Practise finding different letters in the notices.

Writing: Ask the children to draw themselves at the beach or having fun at home and to write about the picture. Help the children hear and write the sounds in the words they need.

Independent activities

1: Listen to the story tape or use Stage I workbooks.

2: Put Sequencing Cards (from Sequencing Cards Photocopy Masters) in order and match captions or write own text.

Group Activity Sheets Book I: Use the notes on page 33 to introduce the following:

3: Word work (page 34) using letters of the alphabet in lower and upper case.

4: Sentence work (page 35) to expect written text to make sense.

5: Text work (page 36) to understand use of the term *letter*.

6: Handwriting: Practise writing capital letters with straight lines (A, E, F, etc.).

Plenary

Use this time to allow children to explain their work to others. It is also an opportunity to reinforce teaching points as they arise and to add to the morning's word work.

Suggested Weekly Plan — FUN AT THE BEACH — STAGE 1 FIRST WORDS — YEAR R

	Whole class – shared reading and writing.	Whole class – phonics, spelling, vocabulary, grammar.	Guided group tasks (reading or writing)	Guided group tasks (reading or writing)	Independent group tasks			Plenary
Mon	Read extended story, letting children read text on each page.	Use magnetic letters in lower case and capitals. Put lower case alphabet in order; match capital letter alphabet.	**Group A** Guided reading. Match upper/lower case letters, GAS Bk1 p34. (T)	**Group B** Story tape, or workbooks. Guided reading or writing. (T)	**Group C** Handwriting. Straight line patterns and capital letters A, E, F, H. (I)	**Group D** Missing words, GAS Bk1 p35. (I)	**Group E** Understand letter, GAS Bk1 p36. (OA)	**Groups D and E** Show work. Play game matching lower case/capital letters.
Tues	Read story, ask children suggested questions, talk about own experiences.	Give out all 26 lower case letters. Show capitals one at a time. Children claim letter to match one held.	**Group E** As above (T)	**Group A** As above (T)	**Group B** As above (I)	**Group C** As above (I)	**Group D** As above (OA)	**Groups B and C** Show work. Use capital letter cards for recognition games.
Wed	Read story together. Read all the notices.	Change GRAND PIER to lower case. Change other notices to capitals.	**Group D** As above (T)	**Group E** As above (T)	**Group A** As above (I)	**Group B** Word lotto Stage 4 or 5, Games Box 4–5. (I)	**Group C** As above (OA)	**Group A** Show work. Read notices in classroom.
Thur	Children suggest words to add to each page, e.g. '... were on the pier.' Teacher scribes.	Revise initial letter sounds using pictures, objects, or games.	**Group C** As group A (T)	**Group D** As above (T)	**Group E** As above (I)	**Group A** As above (I)	**Group B** As above (OA)	Find given words on notices, e.g. find please. Read new captions in story.
Fri	Read new captions together. Read notices in the story and in classroom.	Practise/revise this week's high frequency words or letter sounds.	**Group B** As above (T)	**Group C** As above (T)	**Group D** As above (I)	**Group E** As above (I)	**Group A** As above (OA)	Play matching game as Tuesday word work.

Fitting in with the National Literacy Framework

Word work: W3 sounding and naming letters in lower and upper case; W2 hearing and identifying initial sounds in words.

Sentence work: S1 to expect written text to make sense and to check for sense if it does not.

Text work: T1 to understand and use the term letter; T11 to distinguish between writing and drawing in books.

T = Teacher I = Independent OA = Other adult

These weekly plans are intended as exemplars only and teachers will want to exercise their own skill and judgement when planning for the Literacy Hour.

Stage 2   The Toys' Party   Year R
Stage 2 Wrens   Good Old Mum   Year R

Shared reading and writing

Monday: *The Toys' Party*: Look at the title, cover, and pictures and predict the story. Use the questions to help children to predict the text. Read the text together.

Tuesday: *The Toys' Party*: Recall story before opening book. Read story together. Talk about own cooking at home. Find these key words: *He, put, was*. Use Context Cards to practise reading them.

Wednesday: *Good Old Mum*: Look at the title, cover, and pictures, and predict the story. Read the extended story. Read the text together. Use the pictures to read the last words in each sentence.

Thursday: *The Toys' Party*: take turns to read the text, touching the words one by one while reading. Turn the pages independently. Ask the questions from the extended story.

Friday: *The Toys' Party*: Look at some cookery books for how recipes are written. Shared writing: Write the recipe for Kipper's cake using the ingredients listed in the story.

Word work

Sight recognition of high frequency words and key words from Stage 2.

Monday: Practise recognizing *He, was, put* as single words out of context. (You could use Context Cards for this.) Then find the words in the text and read the sentences.

Tuesday: Revise yesterday's words and others already learned from Stage 1. Make the words with magnetic letters, read them on cards, find them in the text.

Wednesday: Find *put* and *big* on every page. Practise reading and spelling *big, put, was*, and *he*.

Thursday: Cover *He, put*, and *was* in the text. Children predict and spell missing words.

Friday: Practise reading, writing, and spelling this week's high frequency words or letter sounds.

Guided group tasks (reading or writing)

Reading: Talk about the pictures and why Mum looks cross at the end of the book. Why is that? Read the extended story. Read the text independently. Find particular parts of the story, e.g. where Kipper got his toys, when he put in milk. Read those pages.

Writing: Write 'He put in ... ' sentences. Refer to the book to find missing words. Draw the pictures.

Independent activities

1: Listen to the story tape, talking stories, or use Stage 2 workbooks.

2: Choose from a selection of familiar books to read.

Group Activity Sheets Book 1: Use the notes on page 37 to introduce the following:

3: Word work (page 38) for identifying and writing initial phonemes in CVC words.

4: Sentence work (page 39) to expect written text to make sense.

5: Text work (page 40) to reread frequently a familiar text.
Good Old Mum: Pages 41–44 provide activities for children reading this book.

6: *Teacher's Guide 1*: Colouring game explained on page 138 using Activity Sheet 2.18.

Plenary

Use this time to allow children to explain their work to others. It is also an opportunity to reinforce teaching points as they arise and to add to the morning's word work.

Suggested Weekly Plan

THE TOYS' PARTY (STAGE 2) and GOOD OLD MUM (STAGE 2 WRENS) YEAR R

	Whole class – shared reading and writing.	Whole class – phonics, spelling, vocabulary, grammar.	Guided group tasks (reading or writing)	Guided group tasks (reading or writing)	Independent group tasks			Plenary
Mon	*The Toys' Party.* Look at the cover and the pictures. Ask the questions suggested. Read the extended story.	Look at *He, put, was* as single words. Look at length and initial sound. Find the words in the text.	**Group A** Guided reading. Sentences, GAS Bk1 p39.	**Group B** Story tape, talking stories, or workbook. Guided reading or writing. **T**	**Group C** Word recognition practice. Colouring game, TGI p138 AS 2.18. **I**	**Group D** Read familiar stories independently. **I**	**Group E** Initial sounds, GAS Bk1 p38. **OA**	**Group C** Explain colouring game. Read context cards. Look at initial sound of each word.
Tues	*The Toys' Party.* Recall story before opening book. Read the story. Find the key words in the story.	Ask children to find *He, put,* and *was* in the text. Read context cards.	**Group E** As above or *Good Old Mum,* GAS Bk1 p44.	**Group A** As above. **T**	**Group B** As above. **I**	**Group C** As above. **I**	**Group D** As above. **OA**	**Group E** Show work. Make up more sentences with *put.*
Wed	*Good Old Mum.* Look at pictures, read extended story. Read text predicting last words by reference to picture.	Look for *put, big* on each page. Identify initial sound of *big, put, He, was.* Practise reading words on sight.	**Group D** As above.	**Group E** As above. **T**	**Group A** As above. **I**	**Group B** Word lotto Stage 4 or 5, Games Box 4–5. **I**	**Group C** As above. **OA**	**Group D** Talk about favourite story chosen from familiar selection.
Thur	*The Toys' Party.* Take turns to read text, touching words one by one and turning pages.	Cover *He, put,* and *was* in text. Ask children to predict missing words.	**Group C** As group A.	**Group D** As above. **T**	**Group E** As above or key words game, Games Box 1–3. **I**	**Group A** As above. **I**	**Group B** As above. **OA**	**Group A** As above.
Fri	*The Toys' Party.* Write the recipe for Kipper's cake. (Look at cookery books for layout.)	Practise or revise his week's high frequency words or letter sounds.	**Group B** As above.	**Group C** As above. **T**	**Group D** As above. **I**	**Group E** As above. **I**	**Group A** As above. **OA**	**Group B** Read correct sentences. Discuss order of making the cake.

Fitting in with the National Literacy Framework

Word work: W2 identifying and writing initial phonemes in CVC words; **W7** to read on sight the words from texts of appropriate difficulty.

Sentence work: S1 to expect written text to make sense and to check for sense if it does not.

Text work: T6 to reread familiar text; **T1** to track the text in right order, page by page, left to right, pointing while reading and making one to one correspondences between written and spoken words. **T8** to locate and read significant parts of the text. **T15** to use writing to communicate in a variety of ways.

T = Teacher   **I = Independent**   **OA = Other adult**

These weekly plans are intended as exemplars only and teachers will want to exercise their own skill and judgement when planning for the Literacy Hour.

Stage 2 — New Trainers — Year R
Stage 2 Wrens — Fancy Dress — Year R

Shared reading and writing

Monday: *New Trainers*: Look at the title, cover, and pictures and predict the story. Talk about buying new shoes. Use questions to help children predict the text. Read the text together.

Tuesday: *New Trainers*: Read story together. Make clear one to one correspondence of printed and spoken words. Find these key words: *got, to, cross*. Use Context Cards to practise reading them.

Wednesday: *Fancy Dress*: Introduce the book. Read the extended story. Talk about what to do when you come to a word you do not know. Read the text together.

Thursday: *New Trainers*: Use post-it notes to cover key words. Children to predict and spell missing words.

Friday: *New Trainers*: Shared writing: attach speech bubbles to the illustrations. Discuss what the characters are saying. The teacher writes in the speech bubbles.

Word work

Consolidate alphabet in lower case and in capital letters; spell high frequency words; practise identifying families of rhyming CVC words.

Monday: Match lower case and capital letters using cards or magnetic letters. Play I-spy using clothes children are wearing.

Tuesday: Sing or say alphabet. Children find words starting with certain letters (letter names and sounds.).

Wednesday: Make lists of rhyming word families by changing the onset in CVC words. Use CVC words to begin lists using each vowel, e.g. *hat, bed, sit, dog, mug*.

Thursday: Show children how to try out spellings when you are not sure. Does it have the right phonemes? Does it look right? Practise spelling CVC words.

Friday: Practise reading, writing, and spelling this week's high frequency words and spelling patterns.

Guided group tasks (reading or writing)

Reading: Talk about buying new shoes. Why was Dad cross? Read the extended story. Read the text independently. Respond to any difficulties. Encourage the children to use the context to work out new words.

Writing: Use Sequencing Cards for *New Trainers*. Ask children to write their own sentences to match each picture. Help children to hear and write sounds to spell words they need, and to find words in the story.

Independent activities

1 Listen to the story tape, talking stories, or use Stage 2 workbooks.

Group Activity Sheets Book 1: Use the notes on page 45 to introduce the following:

2: Word work (page 46) to understand alphabetical order.

3: Sentence work (page 47) to expect written text to make sense.

4: Text work (page 48) to be aware of story structures.
Fancy Dress: Pages 49–52 provide activities for children reading this book.

5: *Teacher's Guide 1*: Colouring game explained on page 138, Activity Sheet 2.17.

Plenary

Use this time to allow children to explain their work to others. It is also an opportunity to reinforce teaching points as they arise and to add to the morning's word work.

Suggested Weekly Plan — NEW TRAINERS (STAGE 2) and FANCY DRESS (STAGE 2 WRENS) — YEAR R

Day	Whole class – shared reading and writing.	Whole class – phonics, spelling, vocabulary, grammar.	Guided group tasks (reading or writing)	Guided group tasks (reading or writing)	Independent group tasks			Plenary
Mon	New Trainers. Talk about title and cover. Talk about experiences of new clothes. Read extended story.	Sing or say alphabet in order. Play I-spy using clothes the children are wearing.	**Group A** (most able) Guided reading. Why was dad cross? GAS Bk1 p48. **T**	**Group B** Story tape, talking stories, or workbook. Guided reading or writing. **T**	**Group C** Key word recognition. Colouring game. TG1 p138 AS 2.17. **I**	**Group D** Correcting sentences, GAS Bk1 p47 or lotto from Games Box 1–3.	**Group E** Alphabetical order, GAS Bk1 p46, then handwriting – capital letters. **OA**	**Group A** Show work. Find and read sentences in the story.
Tues	New Trainers. Read the story, match written and spoken words. Find key words in the story.	Sing or say alphabet. Teacher asks child to 'find a word beginning with ...' in the text.	**Group E** As above or read Fancy Dress, then GAS Bk1 p 52. **T**	**Group A** As above **T**	**Group B** As above **I**	**Group C** As above	**Group D** As above **OA**	**Group B** Explain colouring game. Read context cards. Put in order.
Wed	Read Fancy Dress. together. Talk about what to do when you meet a new word.	Revise families of rhyming CVC words. Start with hat and cap.	**Group D** As above **T**	**GroupE** As above **T**	**Group A** As above **I**	**Group B** As above	**Group C** As above **OA**	Reread Fancy Dress. Use picture/phonics to read last word in sentences.
Thur	New Trainers. Cover a key word on each page. Predict and spell missing words.	Practise spelling CVC words. Check phonics. Does it look right!	**Group C** As group A **T**	**GroupD** As above **T**	**Group E** As above or rhyming words, GAS Bk1 p50. **I**	**Group A** As above	**Group B** As above **OA**	**Groups C and D** Spell high frequency words chosen by the teacher.
Fri	New Trainers. Attach speech bubbles, discuss, and write what characters say.	Practise/revise this week's high frequency words or letter sounds.	**Group B** As above **T**	**Group C** As above **T**	**Group D** As above **I**	**Group E** As above	**Group A** As above **OA**	**Group E** Show work or explain game to class.

Fitting in with the National Literacy Framework

Word work: W3 understanding alphabetical order; **W2** identifying and writing initial and dominant phonemes in spoken words.

Sentence work: S1 to expect written text to make sense and to check for sense if it does not.

Text work: T9 to be aware of story structures; **T1** to track the text in the right order; page by page, left to right, pointing while reading and making one to one correspondence between written and spoken words. **T11** to understand that writing remains constant.

T = Teacher   **I = Independent**   **OA = Other adult**

These weekly plans are intended as exemplars only and teachers will want to exercise their own skill and judgement when planning for the Literacy Hour.

Stage 2   A New Dog   Year R
Stage 2 Wrens   The Pet Shop   Year R

Shared reading and writing

Monday: *A New Dog*: Look at the title, cover, and pictures, and predict the story. Read the extended story and read the text while pointing to each word.

Tuesday: *A New Dog*: Use questions from extended story to help children predict text. Read together pointing to printed word as it spoken. Find these key words: *They, wanted, Everyone*. Use Context Cards to practise reading them.

Wednesday: *The Pet Shop*: Introduce the book. Read the extended story. Talk about what to do when you come to a word you do not know. Read the text together.

Thursday: *A New Dog*: Retell story from memory. Ask children about their own dogs. Take turns to point to the words as everyone reads.

Friday: *A New Dog*: Shared writing: Children retell story. Children use sounds to help teacher spell words.

Word work

Awareness of alliteration; more rhyming CVC words.

Monday: Introduce the idea of alliteration – matching initial sounds in words by thinking of names and words to match the dogs in the Dogs' Home, e.g. big Ben, little Lucy, hairy Harry etc. Look at the dogs on the cover. Think of names and matching words for some of them.

Tuesday: Add pleasant adjectives to children's names, e.g. cuddly Kipper, beautiful Biff, cheerful Chip, wonderful Wilf, wise Wilma.

Wednesday: Practise spelling more rhyming word families by changing the onset in CVC words. Find more words using each vowel, e.g. *hat, bed, sit, dog, mug*.

Thursday: Practise reading and spelling high frequency words from the text.

Friday: Practise reading, writing, and spelling this week's high frequency words and spelling patterns.

Guided group tasks (reading or writing)

Reading: Talk about the story and how to choose a dog. Read the text independently. Show children how to miss out a word and read on, then reread to help you to work out a new word.

Writing: Use lists of rhyming word families to help children to form letters correctly.

Independent activities

1: Listen to the story tape, talking stories, or use Stage 2 workbooks.

Group Activity Sheets Book 1: Use the notes on page 53 to introduce the following:

2: Word work (page 54) to identify alliteration.

3: Sentence work (page 55) to use the grammar of a sentence to predict words.

4: Text work (page 56) to experiment with writing in a variety of situations.
The Pet Shop: Pages 57–60 provide activities for children reading this book.

5: Sequencing Cards: Ask the children to match the text or write captions independently.

Plenary

Use this time to allow children to explain their work to others. It is also an opportunity to reinforce teaching points as they arise and to add to the morning's word work.

Suggested Weekly Plan   A NEW DOG (STAGE 2) and THE PET SHOP (STAGE 2 WRENS)   YEAR R

	Whole class – shared reading and writing.	Whole class – phonics, spelling, vocabulary, grammar.	Guided group tasks (reading or writing)	Guided group tasks (reading or writing)	Independent group tasks			Plenary
Mon	A New Dog. Talk about title and cover illustration. Read extended story and ask questions.	Alliteration. Invent names for dogs in story matching the sound of the adjective, e.g. big Ben; little Lucy.	**Group A** Guided reading. Write thoughts in speech bubbles, GAS Bk1 p56. [T]	**Group B** Story tape, talking stories, or workbook. Guided reading or writing. [T]	**Group C** Missing words, GAS Bk1 p55, or sentences, 'The train' TG1 AS 2.27. [I]	**Group D** Stories with Sequencing Cards. Match or write text independently. [I]	**Group E** Discuss alliteration, GAS Bk1 p54. Adult helps. [OA]	**Group D** Read own story sequences.
Tues	A New Dog. Recall and retell story together before rereading the text. Find key words in the story.	Reread names and adjectives from yesterday. Add alliterative adjective to children's names.	**Group E** As above or if using The Pet Shop 'Oh no!' or 'Oh yes!' GAS Bk1 p60. [T]	**Group A** As above. [T]	**Group B** As above. [I]	**Group C** As above. [I]	**Group D** As above. [OA]	**Group C** Show work. Practise high frequency words.
Wed	The Pet Shop. Talk about cover and predict story. Read extended story. Read text together.	CVC words using each vowel in turn. Change onsets to spell rhyming families.	**Group D** As above. [T]	**Group E** As above. [T]	**Group A** As above. [I]	**Group B** Word lotto Stage 4 or 5, Games Box 4–5. [I]	**Group C** As above. [OA]	*The Pet Shop.* Alliteration – match adjectives to *rat, spider, snake, goldfish.*
Thur	A New Dog. Take turns to point to words as others read.	Practise reading and spelling high frequency words from the text.	**Group C** As group A [T]	**Group D** As above [T]	**Group E** As above or Rhyming words, GAS Bk1 p58. [I]	**GroupA** As above [I]	**Group B** As above [OA]	**Group A** Read own stories. **Group B** Read alliteration sheets.
Fri	A New Dog. Children retell story. Teacher scribes. Check for consistency.	Practise/revise this week's high frequency words or letter sounds.	**Group B** As above [T]	**Group C** As above [T]	**Group D** As above [I]	**Group E** As above [I]	**Group A** As above [OA]	**Group E** Show and read stories. Reread class story of A New Dog.

Fitting in with the National Literacy Framework

Word work: W4 identifying alliteration in known and new and invented words; **W1** extending rhyming patterns by analogy, generating new and invented words in speech and spelling.

Sentence work: S2 to use awareness of the grammar of a sentence to predict words.

Text work: T12 to experiment with writing in a variety of situations; **T12** to write sentences to match sequences of pictures; **T1** to track text, pointing and making one to one correspondence between written and spoken text.

OA = Other adult

T = Teacher   **I = Independent**   **OA = Other adult**

These weekly plans are intended as exemplars only and teachers will want to exercise their own skill and judgement when planning for the Literacy Hour.

Stage 2   What a Bad Dog! Year R
Stage 2 Wrens   Push!   Year R

Shared reading and writing

Monday: *What a Bad Dog!*: Look at the title, cover, and pictures and predict the story. Use the questions to help children to predict the text. Read the text together.

Tuesday: *What a Bad Dog!*: Recall the story. Use questions that involve children's own thoughts and ideas. Read text together, using a pointer. Find these key words in the story: *in, pulled, pushed*. Use Context Cards to practise reading them.

Wednesday: *Push!*: Introduce the book. Read the extended story. Talk about what to do when you come to a word you do not know. Read the text together.

Thursday: *What a Bad Dog!*: Take turns to read and point to the words. Talk about dogs that misbehave.

Friday: *What a Bad Dog!*: Shared writing: Change all the things Floppy knocked over or pulled down. Teacher scribes children's ideas. Involve children in deciding which letter words begin with.

Word work

Discriminate 'onsets' from 'rimes'; use grammar to predict missing words.

Monday: Use *bad* and *dog* to change onsets and generate more words. Ask children to spell the words they suggest.

Tuesday: Show the children that changing the onset of longer words such as *went* or *sleep* generates rhyming words that we can spell easily.

Wednesday: Use words from the story such as *car* and *and* to generate more rhyming words.

Thursday: Use sentences on Context Cards to put the events in order. Read key words on the reverse.

Friday: Practise reading, writing, and spelling this week's high frequency words and spelling patterns.

Guided group tasks (reading or writing)

Reading: Talk about the cover and the pictures. Predict the story in own words. Listen while the children read independently. Show children how the grammar of a sentence helps us to predict new words.

Writing: Use Sequencing Cards. Ask the children to write a sentence to match each picture. Help them to use phonics and patterns they know to spell the words.

Independent activities

1: Listen to the story tape, talking stories, or use Stage 2 workbooks.

Group Activity Sheets Book 1: Use the notes on page 61 to introduce the following:

2: Word work (page 62) to change the onset to make rhyming words.

3: Sentence work (page 63) to use the grammar of a sentence to predict words.

4: Text work (page 64) to locate and read significant parts of the text.
   Push!: Pages 65–68 provide activities for children reading this book.

5: Handwriting practice: Children working with an adult practise spelling patterns using the correct pencil grip and letter formation.

Plenary

Use this time to allow children to explain their work to others. It is also an opportunity to reinforce teaching points as they arise and to add to the morning's word work.

WHAT A BAD DOG (STAGE 2) and PUSH! (STAGE 2 WRENS) YEAR R

Suggested Weekly Plan

	Whole class – shared reading and writing.	Whole class – phonics, spelling, vocabulary, grammar.	Guided group tasks (reading or writing)	Guided group tasks (reading or writing)	Independent group tasks			Plenary
Mon	*What a Bad Dog!* Use title, cover, and pictures to predict story. Read extended story. Children read text.	Onset and rime. Use *bad* and *dog* to change onset and generate lists of rhyming words.	**Group A** Guided reading. Rhyming words, GAS Bk1 p42. T	**Group B** Story tape, talking stories or workbook. Guided reading or writing. T	**Group C** What did they say? GAS Bk1 p64.	**Group D** Missing words in sentences, GAS Bk1 p59.	**Group E** Handwriting. Correct letter formation. OA	**Group E** Show handwriting. All discuss more rhymes and write lists on board.
Tues	*What a Bad Dog!* Recall story and use questions from extended story. Read text together Find key words.	Reread yesterday's lists. Change onsets for *went*, *sleep*, and *tray* and make lists.	**Group E** As above or read *Push!* then missing words, GAS Bk1 p67. T	**Group A** As above. T	**Group B** As above.	**Group C** As above.	**Group D** As above. OA	**Group C** Explain missing words in sentences.
Wed	*Push!* Predict story from title, cover and pictures. Read extended story. Children read text.	Change onset for *car* and list words made. Add onsets to 'and', make list.	**Group D** As above. T	**Group E** As above.	**Group A** As above.	**Group B** Word lotto Stage 4 or 5, Games Box Stages 4 and 5.	**Group C** As above. OA	Reread *Push!* together. Read and add to lists of rhyming words.
Thur	*What a Bad Dog!* Individuals read different pages, pointing to words as they read.	Cover words in sentences. Show children how knowing grammar helps to predict missing words.	**Group C** As Group A. T	**Group D** As above. T	**Group E** As above or word recognition, GAS Bk1 p66.	**Group A** As above.	**Group B** As above. OA	**Group B** Show handwriting. **Group A** Read sentences.
Fri	*What a Bad Dog!* Change pages 1–7, what Floppy went in and what he pulled and pushed.	Practise/revise this week's high frequency words or letter sounds.	**Group B** As Group A. T	**Group C** As above. T	**Group D** As above.	**Group E** As above.	**Group A** As above. OA	**Group D** Explain 'What did they say?' work.

Fitting in with the National Literacy Framework

Word work: W4 discriminating 'onsets' from 'rimes' in spelling; **W7** to read on sight words from texts of appropriate difficulty; **W14** to write letters using the correct sequence of movements.

Sentence work: S2 to use awareness of the grammar of a sentence to predict words.

Text work: T8 to locate and read significant parts of the text; **T14** to use experience of stories as a basis for writing through substitution through shared composition with adults.

T = Teacher   I = Independent   OA = Other adult

These weekly plans are intended as exemplars only and teachers will want to exercise their own skill and judgement when planning for the Literacy Hour.

Stage 2   The Go-Kart   Year R
Stage 2 Wrens   The Headache   Year R

Shared reading and writing

Monday: *The Go-Kart*: Predict story from the cover and the pictures. Read the extended story. Use the questions to help children to predict the text. Read the text.

Tuesday: *The Go-Kart*: Recall the story. Use questions that involve children's own thoughts and ideas. Read text together, using a pointer. Find these key words in the story: *made*, *said*, *had*. Use Context Cards to practise reading them.

Wednesday: *The Headache*: Introduce the book. Read the extended story. Talk about what to do when you come to a word you do not know. Read the text together.

Thursday: *The Go-Kart*: Read and point to words. Use pictures, phonics, or context to decode a new word.

Friday: *The Go-Kart*: Shared writing: What are Mum and Dad saying or thinking when the children quarrel? Children suggest ideas for the teacher to write. Attach the speech bubbles to the book.

Word work

High frequency words from the list for Year R; identify initial and dominant phonemes in simple words.

Monday: Cover verbs in the story. Ask children to use the sense of the story to predict the missing words.

Tuesday: Cover the same verbs as yesterday. Ask the children to identify the initial and dominant phonemes in the words. Spell them together.

Wednesday: Cover last words on each page. Children use the sense of the sentence to predict the missing word. Identify initial and dominant phonemes to help to spell the words.

Thursday: Practise identifying the phonemes in high frequency words for Year R. Spell them together.

Friday: Practise reading, writing, and spelling this week's high frequency words and spelling patterns.

Guided group tasks (reading or writing)

Reading: Talk about the cover and pictures. Predict the story in own words. Listen to children reading independently. Remind children of strategies to cope with new words.

Writing: Use spelling patterns to help children practise correct letter formation.

Independent activities

1: Listen to the story tape, talking stories, or use Stage 2 workbooks.

Group Activity Sheets Book 1: Use the notes on page 69 to introduce the following:

2: Word work (page 70) to read on sight high frequency words to be taught by the end of Year R. If time, play a word game from Games Box Stages 1–3.

3: Sentence work (page 71) so that words are ordered left to right and need to be read that way to make sense.

4: Text work (page 72) to write sentences to match pictures.
The Headache: Pages 73–76 provide activities for children reading this book.

5: Familiar books for children to read.

Plenary

Use this time to allow children to explain their work to others. It is also an opportunity to reinforce teaching points as they arise and to add to the morning's word work.

Suggested Weekly Plan — THE GO-KART (STAGE 2) and THE HEADACHE (STAGE 2 WRENS) — YEAR R

Day	Whole class – shared reading and writing	Whole class – phonics, spelling, vocabulary, grammar	Guided group tasks (reading or writing)	Guided group tasks (reading or writing)	Independent group tasks	Plenary
Mon	*The Go-Kart.* Predict story from title, cover, and pictures. Read extended story. Children read text.	Cover verbs and ask children to predict using the sense of the sentence. Use phonics to check.	**Group A** Guided reading. Adapt the story using GAS Bk1 p72. [T]	**Group B** Story tape, talking story, or workbook. Guided reading or writing. [T]	**Group C** Word order in sentences GAS Bk1 p71. [I] **Group D** Choose from familiar books to reread in pairs or independently. [I] **Group E** Familiar words, GAS Bk1 p70. Lotto game, Games Box 1–3. [OA]	**Group C** Read sentences with correct word order.
Tues	*The Go-Kart.* Use questions from extended story. Find key words in the story.	As above but ask children to use phonic knowledge to spell the missing words.	**Group E** As above or read *The Headache* TG1 p138 AS 2.25, 2.26. [T]	**Group A** As above [T]	**Group B** As above [I] **Group C** As above [I] **Group D** As above [OA]	**Group D** Explain their word work.
Wed	*The Headache.* Predict story from title, cover, and pictures. Read extended story. Read text together.	Cover last word on each page. Use picture to predict. Check first and last letters, phonemes and length of word.	**Group D** As above [T]	**Group E** As above [T]	**Group A** As above [I] **Group B** As above [I] **Group C** As above [OA]	**Group B** Talk about books chosen to read.
Thur	*The Go-Kart.* Individual children read. Use a variety of cues for unknown words.	Practise identifying phonemes in simple words. Discuss how to write them.	**Group C** As above [T]	**Group D** As above [T]	**Group E** As above or *The Headache*, GAS Bk1 p76. [I] **Group A** As above [I] **Group B** As above [OA]	**Group E** Read sentences.
Fri	*The Go-Kart.* Use speech bubbles to add what Dad and Mum are saying/thinking.	Practise/revise this week's high frequency words or letter sounds.	**Group B** As above [T]	**Group C** As above [T]	**Group D** As above [I] **Group E** As above [I] **Group A** As above [OA]	**Group A** Read sentences with words from garage door.

Fitting in with the National Literacy Framework

Word work: W6 to read on sight high frequency words from the Year R list; **W2** identifying and writing initial and dominant phonemes in spoken words.

Sentence work: S3 that words are ordered left to right and need to be read that way to make sense.

Text work: T12 to write sentences to match pictures; **T2** to use a variety of cues when reading.

T = Teacher   **I = Independent**   **OA = Other adult**

These weekly plans are intended as exemplars only and teachers will want to exercise their own skill and judgement when planning for the Literacy Hour.

Stage 2   The Dream   Year R
Stage 2 Wrens   At the Park   Year R

Shared reading and writing

Monday: *The Dream*: Predict story from the cover and the pictures. Read the extended story. Use questions to help children predict the text. Read text together.

Tuesday: *The Dream*: Recall the story. Use questions that involve children's own thoughts and ideas. Talk about children's own dreams. Read text together. Find these key words in the story: *It, it, went*. Use Context Cards to practise reading them.

Wednesday: *At the Park*: Introduce book. Read extended story. Read text together. Look for *went, on, the* on each page.

Thursday: *The Dream*: Read and point to the words. Use picture, phonics, or context to decode a new word.

Friday: *The Dream*: Shared writing: make up the story Mum told Biff, but change dolphin to something that would not frighten her. The teacher writes the story using the children's suggestions.

Word work

Recognize Stage 2 key words; notice the shape and length of words.

Monday: Cover words with silhouettes that show ascenders and descenders. Predict missing words and check them by matching them to the shapes.

Tuesday: Cover some more words with silhouettes and predict the missing words using the shape as a clue. Match children's names to their silhouettes.

Wednesday: Cover the last word in each sentence with a silhouette. Discuss and draw the shapes of words suggested to check that they fit before looking at the text.

Thursday: Practise recognition of all Stage 2 key words.

Friday: Practise reading, writing, and spelling this week's high frequency words and spelling patterns.

Guided group tasks (reading or writing)

Reading: Talk about the cover and the pictures. Predict the story in own words. Remind children to point to words as they read to match spoken and written words.

Writing: Use Sequencing Cards for *At the Park* or for *The Dream*. Ask children to write the story themselves. Notice strategies for spelling independently. You could use the stories as an assessment.

Independent activities

1: Listen to the story tape, talking stories, or use Stage 2 workbooks.

Group Activity Sheets Book 1: Use the notes on page 77 to introduce the following:

2: Word work (page 78) to recognize the critical features of words, e.g. shape.

3: Sentence work (page 79) so that words are ordered left to right and need to be read that way to make sense.

4: Text work (page 80) to use experience of stories as a basis for independent writing.
At the Park: Pages 81–84 provide activities for children reading this book.

5: Handwriting practise: Patterns and spelling patterns to copy.

Plenary

Use this time to allow children to explain their work to others. It is also an opportunity to reinforce teaching points as they arise and to add to the morning's word work.

Suggested Weekly Plan — YEAR R

THE DREAM (STAGE 2) and AT THE PARK (STAGE 2 WRENS)

	Whole class – shared reading and writing.	Whole class – phonics, spelling, vocabulary, grammar.	Guided group tasks (reading or writing)	Guided group tasks (reading or writing)	Independent group tasks	Independent group tasks	Independent group tasks	Plenary
Mon	*The Dream.* Predict story from title, cover, and pictures. Read extended story. Children read text.	Cover some words with silhouettes that show ascenders and descenders. Children predict words from shape.	**Group A** Guided reading. First and last words, GAS Bk1 p79. (T)	**Group B** Story tape, talking story, or workbook. Guided reading or writing. (T)	**Group C** The dolphin story, GAS Bk1 p80. (I)	**Group D** Handwriting patterns and letter formation, e.g. *had, Dad.* (I)	**Group E** Word shapes, GAS Bk1 p78. Draw some more. (OA)	**Group E** Explain matching words to their shapes.
Tues	*The Dream.* Use questions from extended story. Find key words in the story.	Predict more words from their shape. Predict children's names from the shape.	**Group E** As above or read *At the Park.* Length of words, GAS Bk1 p82. (T)	**Group A** As above (T)	**Group B** As above (I)	**Group C** As above (I)	**Group D** As above (OA)	**Group C** Show and explain handwriting patterns.
Wed	*At the Park.* Predict story from title, cover, and pictures. Read extended story. Read text together.	Cover last word in each sentence with a word silhouette. Discuss shape of first and last letters to see if they fit.	**Group D** As above (T)	**Group E** As above (T)	**Group A** As above (I)	**Group B** As above (I)	**Group C** As above (OA)	**Group A** Read story of the dolphin dream. **Group D** Read and explain sentence work.
Thur	*The Dream.* Children read text. Check 1:1 correspondence of printed and spoken words.	Practise all Stage 2 words or all Year R words using flash cards or GAS Bk1 pp117 and 125 (enlarged).	**Group C** As above (T)	**Group D** As above (T)	**Group E** As above or *At the Park* sentences, GAS Bk1 p83. (I)	**Group A** As above (I)	**Group B** As above (OA)	Match more words to their shapes.
Fri	*The Dream.* Change the 'dolphin' to another idea. Invent new story that Mum told Biff.	Practise/revise this week's high frequency words or letter sounds.	**Group B** As above (T)	**Group C** As above (T)	**Group D** As above (I)	**Group E** As above (OA)	**Group A** As above (OA)	**Group B** Show and explain sentence work.

Fitting in with the National Literacy Framework

Word work: W9 to recognize the critical features of words, e.g. shape; **W7** to read on sight the words from texts of appropriate difficulty.

Sentence work: S3 that words are ordered left to right and need to be read that way to make sense.

Text work: T14 to use experience of stories as a basis for independent writing and through shared composition with adults.

T = Teacher   **I = Independent**   **OA = Other adult**

These weekly plans are intended as exemplars only and teachers will want to exercise their own skill and judgement when planning for the Literacy Hour.

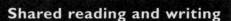

Stage 3　　On the Sand　　Year 1 Term 1

Shared reading and writing

Monday: Predict the story from the cover and the pictures. Read the extended story. Use the questions to help children to predict the text. Read the text together.

Tuesday: Recall the story. Use questions that involve children's own thoughts and ideas. Read text together, using a pointer. Find these key words: *on, looked, at.* Use Context Cards to practise reading them.

Wednesday: Ask children to retell the story in own words. Read text and compare it with the retold version.

Thursday: Reread the story. Talk about own experiences at seaside. Children to speak clearly in whole sentences. Cover *asleep* on page 7. Ask the children how to work out what the missing word could be? How do they know? How could they check? Use pictures, context and phonics to be sure.

Friday: Shared writing: Use children's experiences to write a class 'On the Sand' story. Teacher scribes. Children suggest how to spell common words.

Word work

Revise alphabetical order; consolidate use of rhyme for spelling; practise reading and spelling two- and three-letter words from NLS Framework Appendix List 1.

Monday: Sing or say the alphabet. Play I-spy using initial letters, then 'something ending with …'.

Tuesday: Practise changing onsets to make more rhyming words, e.g. *look, book, took* etc. Or use words on Clue Cards from *Rhyme and Analogy, Teacher's Guide 1* pp108–113 to make rhyming lists of words.

Wednesday: Cover all the three-letter words in the story. Ask children to predict and spell them from memory (was) or using phonics (hat).

Thursday: Practise recognition of two- and three-letter words from Appendix List 1 of the NLS Framework. (These are set out on page 126 of the *Group Activity Sheets Book 1*.)

Friday: Practise reading, writing, and spelling this week's high frequency words and spelling patterns.

Guided group tasks (reading or writing)

Reading: Talk about the cover and the pictures. Predict the story in own words. Look for new words in the text and help each other use a variety of cues to decode them. Remind children to point to words as they read to match spoken and written words.

Writing: Use rhyming words to practise letter formation, e.g. *sand, band, hand* etc.

Independent activities

1: Listen to the story tape, talking stories, or use Stage 3 workbooks.

Group Activity Sheets Book 1: Use the notes on page 85 to introduce the following:

2: Word work (page 86) to practise and secure the ability to rhyme.

3: Sentence work (page 87) to expect written text to make sense.

4: Text work (page 88) to describe story settings and incidents and relate them to own experience and that of others.

5: Sequencing Cards for *On the Sand*: Ask the children to retell the story, matching the sentences provided or writing their own sentences according to ability.

Plenary

Use this time to allow children to explain their work to others. It is also an opportunity to reinforce teaching points as they arise and to add to the morning's word work.

Suggested Weekly Plan　　ON THE SAND　　STAGE 3　　YEAR 1 TERM 1

	Whole class – shared reading and writing.	Whole class – phonics, spelling, vocabulary, grammar.	Guided group tasks (reading or writing)	Guided group tasks (reading or writing)	Independent group tasks	Independent group tasks	Independent group tasks	Plenary
Mon	Predict story from title, cover, and pictures. Read extended text. Children read text.	Sing or say alphabet. Play I-spy using illustrations. If confident change to 'something ending with ...'	**Group A** Guided reading. Rhyming words, GAS Bk1 p86. — T	**Group B** Story tape, talking story, or workbook. Guided reading or writing. — T	**Group C** Use sequencing cards to retell story: match sentences or write own words. — I	**Group D** Sentences must make sense, GAS Bk1 p87. — I	**Group E** Own experiences, GAS Bk1 p88. — OA	**Group E** Explain their work. **Group C** Read stories.
Tues	Use questions from extended story and include children's own experiences. Find key words.	Practise changing onsets to make rhyming words, e.g. look, took, book; sand, hand, land.	**Group E** As above — T	**Group A** As above — T	**Group B** As above — I	**Group C** As above — I	**Group D** As above — OA	**Group B** Read stories. Make more rhyming words and write list.
Wed	Retell the story orally then read text. Notice the difference.	Cover three-letter words. Ask children to predict and spell by using phonemes or from memory.	**Group D** As above — T	**Group E** As above — T	**Group A** As above — I	**Group B** As above — I	**Group C** As above — OA	**Group D** Read rhyming words. **Group A** Read stories.
Thur	Reread story. Talk about experiences at seaside. Cover *asleep*; use cues to work out the missing word.	Practise spelling two- and three-letter words from Appendix List 1. (See GAS Bk1 p126.)	**Group C** As above — T	**Group D** As above — T	**Group E** As above or story to match book from Guided reading. — I	**Group A** As above — I	**Group B** As above — OA	Spell more two and three letter words from Appendix List 1.
Fri	Write a new 'On the Sand' story using children's own experiences.	Practise/revise this week's high frequency words or spelling patterns.	**Group B** As above — T	**Group C** As above — T	**Group D** As above — I	**Group E** As above — I	**Group A** As above — OA	Read new story together.

Fitting in with the National Literacy Framework

Word work: W1 to practise ability to rhyme, and relate to spelling patterns; **W9** to read on sight high frequency words from Appendix List 1; **W3** to practise the ability to hear initial and final phonemes in CVC words.

Sentence work: S1 to expect written text to make sense and to check for sense if it does not.

Text work: T5 to describe story settings and relate to own experiences; **T9** to write about events in personal experience linked to a variety of familiar incidents from stories.

T = Teacher　　　　**I = Independent**　　　　**OA = Other adult**

These weekly plans are intended as exemplars only and teachers will want to exercise their own skill and judgement when planning for the Literacy Hour.

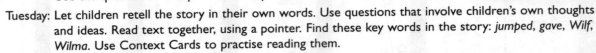

Stage 3   The Dolphin Pool   Year 1 Term 1

The Dolphin Pool
Roderick Hunt   Alex Brychta

Shared reading and writing

Monday: Predict the story from the cover and the pictures. Read the extended story. Use the questions to help children to predict the text. Read the text together.

Tuesday: Let children retell the story in their own words. Use questions that involve children's own thoughts and ideas. Read text together, using a pointer. Find these key words in the story: *jumped, gave, Wilf, Wilma.* Use Context Cards to practise reading them.

Wednesday: Children read text together. Read at normal pace, using expression. Cover *through* on page 5. Show children how to use context, picture, and phonic knowledge to work out what the word is.

Thursday: Use Context Cards. Put them in order. Find matching sentences in story. Read story.

Friday: Shared writing: Change title to 'The Zoo' and make up story of Wilf and Wilma making friends with an animal. Teacher scribes. Children use words from text and phonics to help with spellings.

Word work

Learn to organize words in alphabetical order; practise reading and spelling two- and three-letter words from NLS Framework Appendix List 1.

Monday: Sing or say the alphabet. Show children their names are in alphabetical order in the register. Use three or four first names on cards and put them in alphabetical order. Repeat with different names.

Tuesday: Practise putting more names in alphabetical order. Think of three animal names. Which will come first in the dictionary? Use a picture dictionary to check.

Wednesday: Practise spelling CVC words from Appendix List 1 of the NLS Framework.

Thursday: Practise recognition of two- and three-letter words from Appendix List 1 of the NLS Framework. (See page 126 of the *Group Activity Sheets Book 1.*)

Friday: Practise reading, writing, and spelling this week's high frequency words and spelling patterns.

Guided group tasks (reading or writing)

Reading: Talk about the cover and the pictures. Predict the story in own words. Look for new words in the text and help each other use a variety of cues to decode them. Remind children to point to words as they read to match spoken and written words.

Writing: Review any recent written work. Focus on spelling patterns, letter formation, or punctuation according to need.

Independent activities

1: Listen to the story tape, talking stories, or use Stage 3 workbooks.

Group Activity Sheets Book 1: Use the notes on page 89 to introduce the following:

2: Word work (page 90) to practise and secure alphabetical order.

3: Sentence work (page 91) to write simple sentences and to reread, recognizing whether or not they make sense.

4: Text work (page 92) to read familiar, simple stories independently, to point while reading and make correspondence between words said and read.

5: Choice of familiar books to read or games from Games Box for Stages 1–3.

Plenary

Use this time to allow children to explain their work to others. It is also an opportunity to reinforce teaching points as they arise and to add to the morning's word work.

Suggested Weekly Plan   THE DOLPHIN POOL   STAGE 3   YEAR I TERM I

	Whole class – shared reading and writing.	Whole class – phonics, spelling, vocabulary, grammar.	Guided group tasks (reading or writing)	Guided group tasks (reading or writing)	Independent group tasks			Plenary
Mon	Predict story from title, cover, and pictures. Read extended story. Children read text.	Alphabetical order. Put children or name cards in order, saying and checking for each letter in turn.	**Group A** Guided reading. Writing sentences, GAS Bk1 p91. (T)	**Group B** Story tape, talking story, or workbook. Guided reading or writing. (T)	**Group C** Alphabetical order, GAS Bk1 p90. (I)	**Group D** Game from Games Box 1–3 or familiar books to read. (I)	**Group E** Match 1:1 words said/printed, GAS Bk1 p92. (OA)	Alphabetical names – add or think of names to fit in the gaps. **Group C** Show work.
Tues	Recall story and retell in own words. Children talk about own experiences feeding animals. Find key words in story.	Alphabetical order. Put children or name cards in order, saying and checking for each letter in turn.	**Group E** As above or use sequencing cards to order and match text. (T)	**Group A** As above (T)	**Group B** As above (I)	**Group C** As above (I)	**Group D** As above (OA)	**Group E** Show sentences or story. Add animals to alphabetical order list.
Wed	Children read text, pointing to words as they read. Cover *through* words to use cues to work it out.	Practise spelling *big*, *got*, *wet* and other CVC words, identifying first and last phonemes.	**Group D** As above (T)	**Group E** As above (T)	**Group A** As above (I)	**Group B** Word lotto Stage 4 or 5, Games Box 4–5. (I)	**Group C** As above (OA)	**Group A** Show work and handwriting.
Thur	Read context cards. Put in order, find in book, and match to story.	Practise reading and writing two- and three-letter high frequency words from List 1.	**Group C** As above (T)	**Group D** As above (T)	**Group E** As above or order R&A alphabet cards. (I)	**Group A** As above (I)	**Group B** As above (OA)	**Group B** Show and explain work.
Fri	Change title to 'The Zoo' and change animals, e.g. elephant instead of killer whale.	Practise/revise this week's words from high frequency list.	**Group B** As above (T)	**Group C** As above (T)	**Group D** As above (I)	**Group E** As above (I)	**Group A** As above (OA)	**Group D** Show writing. Read new story together.

Fitting in with the National Literacy Framework

Word work: W2 to practise and secure alphabetic knowledge; **W3** to practise and secure the ability to hear initial and final phonemes in CVC words.

Sentence work: S4 to write simple sentences and to reread recognizing whether or not they make sense.

Text work: T4 to read simple stories independently, to point while reading, and link words said and read; **T8** through shared writing to apply phonological, graphic knowledge, and sight vocabulary to spell words correctly.

T = Teacher   **I = Independent**   **OA = Other adult**

These weekly plans are intended as exemplars only and teachers will want to exercise their own skill and judgement when planning for the Literacy Hour.

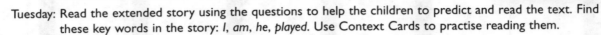

Stage 3 Nobody Wanted to Play Year 1 Term 1

Shared reading and writing

Monday: Predict the story from the cover and the pictures. Read the extended story. Children talk about their own experiences. Read the text together.

Tuesday: Read the extended story using the questions to help the children to predict and read the text. Find these key words in the story: *I, am, he, played.* Use Context Cards to practise reading them.

Wednesday: Cover the item Wilf played on. Children predict from the picture, then use phonics, word length and context to check that they are right.

Thursday: Read together with pace and expression. Cover the picture of spiderman on page 15. Children to give ideas for working out the word without using picture. Use context and phonic knowledge.

Friday: Shared writing: Talk about what children do when nobody wants to play with them. Make list: 'When nobody wants to play you can 1) Find a good book to read. 2) Play a game on your own.'

Word work

Looking for words inside words; vocabulary extension; practise putting words in alphabetical order.

Monday: Find words inside words, e.g. *spaceman.* Find other words in the story that have smaller words inside them. Collect more for a display.

Tuesday: Revise words inside words listed yesterday. Think of or find more to add to the list. Include shorter words, e.g. *he* in *they.*

Wednesday: Vocabulary extension: think of more words for playground equipment.

Thursday: Look at yesterday's list and put the words in alphabetical order. Use the new list as a word bank.

Friday: Practise reading, writing, and spelling this week's high frequency words and spelling patterns.

Guided group tasks (reading or writing)

Reading: Talk about the cover and the pictures. Predict the story in own words. Look for new words in the text and help each other use a variety of cues to decode them. Encourage children to reread sentences that do not seem to make sense.

Writing: Use Sequencing Cards for *Nobody Wanted to Play.* Discuss each picture in turn and write a sentence to match it. Use capital letters and full stops correctly.

Independent activities

1: Listen to the story tape, talking stories, or use Stage 3 workbooks.

Group Activity Sheets Book 1: Use the notes on page 93 to introduce the following:

2: Word work (page 94) to recognize words within words.

3: Sentence work (page 95) to understand that a line of writing is not necessarily the same as a sentence.

4: Text work (page 96) to make lists, to use patterned stories as a model for their own writing.

5: Teacher's Guide 1: Play 'Don't play on the tiger!' game on page 194 using Activity Sheet 3.23.

Plenary

Use this time to allow children to explain their work to others. It is also an opportunity to reinforce teaching points as they arise and to add to the morning's word work.

Suggested Weekly Plan — NOBODY WANTED TO PLAY — STAGE 3 — YEAR 1 TERM 1

	Whole class – shared reading and writing.	Whole class – phonics, spelling, vocabulary, grammar.	Guided group tasks (reading or writing)	Guided group tasks (reading or writing)	Independent group tasks			Plenary
Mon	Predict story from title and cover. Children talk about experiences. Read extended story with text.	Find words with *man*: *spaceman*, *stuntman*, *fireman*, *spiderman*. Think of more and write class list for display	**Group A** Guided reading. Words inside words, GAS Bk1 p94. — T	**Group B** Story tape, talking story or workbook. Guided reading or writing. — T	**Group C** Sensible sentences, GAS Bk1 p95. — I	**Group D** 'Don't play on the tiger!' game TG1 p194 AS 3.23. — I	**Group E** A trip to the park, GAS Bk1 p96. — I	**Group A** Show words inside words work. Add to list of *men* words.
Tues	Read extended story, children read text. Find key words in the story.	Read list of words and add more. Find words inside other words, e.g. *no* in *nobody*.	**Group E** As above or sequencing cards – order and match text. — T	**Group A** As above — T	**Group B** As above — I	**Group C** As above — I	**Group D** As above — OA	**Group B** Read work and explain how to recognize 'sentences' and 'not sentences'. — OA
Wed	Cover the item Wilf played on. Children check prediction using phonics, context, and grammar.	Vocabulary extension. Ask children to list more playground equipment they know about.	**Group D** As above — T	**Group E** As above — T	**Group A** As above — I	**Group B** Word lotto Stage 4 or 5, Games Box 4–5. — I	**Group C** As above — OA	**Group C** Read 'A trip to the park' work. Segment and blend more CVC words. — OA
Thur	Read together, with expression noticing punctuation. Work out *spiderman* without picture.	Rewrite list of play equipment in alphabetical order. Add more items. Use as word bank.	**Group C** As above — T	**Group D** As above — T	**Group E** As above or sentences, TG1 AS 3.17, 3.18. — I	**Group A** As above — I	**Group B** As above — OA	**Group E** Show work. Spell more CVC words. — OA
Fri	Talk about what children do when nobody wants to play with them. Write down replies.	Practise/revise this week's high frequency words or spelling patterns.	**Group B** As above — T	**Group C** As above — T	**Group D** As above — I	**Group E** As above — I	**Group A** As above — OA	Read ideas for playing alone. Add some more. — OA

T = Teacher   I = Independent   OA = Other adult

Fitting in with the National Literacy Framework

Word work: W10 to recognize the critical features of words, e.g. words within words; **W12** new words from reading and from shared experiences; **W2** to practise and secure alphabetical order.

Sentence work: S7 that a line of writing is not necessarily the same as a sentence.
Text work: T15 to make simple lists; **T10** to use phonological, contextual, grammatical, and graphic knowledge to predict and check the meaning of unfamiliar words. **T2** to use patterned stories as models for writing;

These weekly plans are intended as exemplars only and teachers will want to exercise their own skill and judgement when planning for the Literacy Hour.

A Cat in the Tree
Roderick Hunt   Alex Brychta

Stage 3   A Cat in the Tree   Year 1 Term 1

Shared reading and writing

Monday: Predict the story from the cover and the pictures. Read the extended story. Use the questions to help the children to predict the text. Read text together.

Tuesday: Read text together pointing at each word in turn but maintaining natural expression. Find *climbed* and *couldn't* in the text. Ask the children to explain how they know which of the two words it is. Find these key words: *up, down, tree, climbed*. Use Context Cards to practise reading them.

Wednesday: Shared writing: Talk about the sequence of events needed to get a cat out of a tree. Teacher scribes. Revise and number the instructions.

Thursday: Read instructions written yesterday. Use context and phonics to work out and check new words. Are the instructions clear? Would little pictures make them clearer? Children add small pictures.

Friday: Read story together with pace and expression. What would children do if their cat was up a tree?

Word work

Write all three phonemes in CVC words; recognise and use capital letters and full stops in sentences.

Monday: List CVC words that rhyme with *cat* and *dog*. Ask children to spell the words using letter sounds and letter names.

Tuesday: Write CVC words that do not rhyme. Ask children to spell them by segmenting the words into the three phonemes.

Wednesday: Look for capital letters and full stops in the text. Ask children to suggest a sentence with one of the CVC words listed yesterday. Ask them to say where the capital letter and full stop should go.

Thursday: Read through instructions written yesterday. Check capital letters and full stops. Make up some more sentences.

Friday: Practise reading, writing, and spelling this week's high frequency words and spelling patterns.

Guided group tasks (reading or writing)

Reading: Talk about the cover and the pictures. Predict the story in own words. Look for new words in the text and use a variety of cues to decode them. Read the story independently.

Writing: Review any recent piece of written work. Help children to improve content, spelling, or handwriting according to need.

Independent activities

1: Listen to the story tape, talking stories, or use Stage 3 workbooks.

Group Activity Sheets Book 1: Use the notes on page 97 to introduce the following:

2: Word work (page 98) to represent in writing the three phonemes in CVC words.

3: Sentence work (page 99) to recognize capital letters and full stops when reading, and to name them correctly.

4: Text work (page 100) to read and follow simple instructions.

5: Word recognition game: *Teacher's Guide 1* page 195 using Activity Sheet 3.28.

Plenary

Use this time to allow children to explain their work to others. It is also an opportunity to reinforce teaching points as they arise and to add to the morning's word work.

Suggested Weekly Plan — A CAT IN THE TREE — STAGE 3 — YEAR 1 TERM 1

Day	Whole class – shared reading and writing.	Whole class – phonics, spelling, vocabulary, grammar.	Guided group tasks (reading or writing)	Guided group tasks (reading or writing)	Independent group tasks			Plenary
Mon	Predict story from title and cover. Read extended story using questions. Read text.	Make and list CVC words that rhyme with *cat* and *dog*.	**Group A** Guided reading Punctuation, GAS Bk1 p99. (T)	**Group B** Story tape, talking story, or workbook. Guided reading or writing. (T)	**Group C** CVC words, GAS Bk1 p98. (I)	**Group D** Word recognition. The cat in the tree, TG1 p195 AS 3.28. (I)	**Group E** Instructions, GAS Bk1 p100. (OA)	**Group A** Show and explain punctuation work. Make more words to rhyme with *get*.
Tues	Read text together pointing to the words. Find key words in the story.	Make and list CVC words that do not rhyme. Say and segment words to identify phonemes.	**Group E** As above (T)	**Group A** As above (T)	**Group B** As above (I)	**Group C** As above (I)	**Group D** As above (OA)	**Group B** Show CVC words. Read their words and check their spellings.
Wed	Talk about the sequence of events in getting a cat out of a tree. Teacher writes list.	Find capital letters and full stops in the text. Put CVC words listed yesterday into sentences.	**Group D** As above (T)	**Group E** As above (T)	**Group A** As above (I)	**Group B** Word lotto Stage 4 or 5, Games Box 4–5. (I)	**Group C** As above (OA)	**Group C** Show their instructions work. Compare with class instructions.
Thur	Read instructions written yesterday. Are they clear? Children draw small pictures to clarify instructions.	Find capital letters and full stops in instructions. Make up more sentences and use correct punctuation.	**Group C** As above (T)	**Group D** As above (T)	**Group E** As above (I)	**Group A** As above (I)	**Group B** As above (OA)	**Group E** Read and check CVC words on work sheet. Suggest and spell more.
Fri	Read the text together. What would children really do about a cat in a tree?	Practise/revise this week's high frequency words or spelling patterns.	**Group B** As above (T)	**Group C** As above (T)	**Group D** As above (I)	**Group E** As above (I)	**Group A** As above (OA)	**Group D** Show and check CVC words. Read all the words listed this week.

Fitting in with the National Literacy Framework

Word work: W6 to represent in writing the three phonemes in CVC words.

Sentence work: S5 to recognize full stops and capital letters when reading and name them correctly.

Text work: T13 to read and follow simple instructions; **T16** to write and draw simple instructions.

T = Teacher   I = Independent   OA = Other adult

These weekly plans are intended as exemplars only and teachers will want to exercise their own skill and judgement when planning for the Literacy Hour.

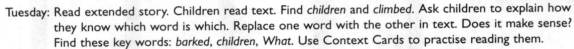

Stage 3   The Rope Swing   Year 1 Term 1

Shared reading and writing

Monday: Predict story from the cover and the pictures. Read the extended story. Use the questions to help the children to predict the text. Read the text together.

Tuesday: Read extended story. Children read text. Find *children* and *climbed*. Ask children to explain how they know which word is which. Replace one word with the other in text. Does it make sense? Find these key words: *barked, children, What*. Use Context Cards to practise reading them.

Wednesday: Ask the children to retell the story, then read the text and compare with the written version.

Thursday: Shared Writing: Decide what Floppy is trying to tell the children. The teacher writes the children's ideas on speech bubbles and attaches them to the pages. Children suggest how to spell the words.

Friday: Take turns to read pages of the story. Read what Floppy is saying. Use appropriate expression. Talk about how the story ends. How could the ending have been different?

Word work

Notice common spelling patterns in words; practise sight recognition of Stage 3 key words.

Monday: Copy spelling of *swing* from the cover of the book. Ask children to think of and spell more words ending in *ing*. The teacher writes a list.

Tuesday: Look at each picture in turn and think of a word that describes what the children are doing, e.g. *walking, climbing* etc. Ask the children to spell the words.

Wednesday: Look for words ending in *ed* in the text. Make a list and ask the children to suggest more.

Thursday: Practise sight recognition of Stage 3 key words learned so far. You could use Context Cards as flash cards.

Friday: Practise reading, writing, and spelling this week's high frequency words and spelling patterns.

Guided group tasks (reading or writing)

Reading: Talk about the cover and the pictures. Predict the story in own words. When reading notice and respond to full stops at the end of sentences. Reread sentences if they do not seem to make sense.

Writing: Talk about things that children need to remember, e.g. things to take home from school. Discuss how to write a list to remind them. Each child writes a list.

Independent activities

1: Listen to the story tape, talking stories, or use Stage 3 workbooks.

Group Activity Sheets Book 1: Use the notes on page 101 to introduce the following:

2: Word work (page 102) to recognize common spelling patterns in words.

3: Sentence work (page 103) to begin using full stops to demarcate sentences.

4: Text work (page 104) to make simple lists for reminding.

5: *Teacher's Guide 1*: Word recognition game on page 195 using Activity Sheet 3.28.

Plenary

Use this time to allow children to explain their work to others. It is also an opportunity to reinforce teaching points as they arise and to add to the morning's word work.

Suggested Weekly Plan   THE ROPE SWING   STAGE 3   YEAR 1 TERM 1

	Whole class – shared reading and writing.	Whole class – phonics, spelling, vocabulary, grammar.	Guided group tasks (reading or writing)	Guided group tasks (reading or writing)	Independent group tasks	Independent group tasks	Independent group tasks	Plenary
Mon	Predict story from title and cover. Read extended story. Ask questions listed. Read text.	Copy spelling of swing from cover. Make and list more words to rhyme with swing.	**Group A** Guided reading. Writing lists, GAS Bk1 p104. T	**Group B** Story tape, talking story, or workbook. Guided reading or writing. T	**Group C** ing words, GAS Bk1 p102. R&A rhyming card games. I	**Group D** As above. Punctuation, GAS Bk1 p103. I	**Group E** Handwriting patterns and correct formation of ing words. OA	**Group C** Show work and read ing words. **Group D** Show punctuation work.
Tues	Read extended story. Children join in reading text, using expression. Find key words in the story.	Look at what is happening in each picture and list ing verbs, e.g. climbing, barking.	**Group E** As above T	**Group A** As above T	**Group B** As above I	**Group C** As above I	**Group D** As above OA	Read list of ing verbs and add some more.
Wed	Retell the story in own words. Compare with text version.	Look for words ending with ed. Make a list and think of more to add.	**Group D** As above T	**Group E** As above T	**Group A** As above I	**Group B** Word lotto Stage 4 or 5, Games Box 4–5. I	**Group C** As above OA	**Group B** Show and explain punctuation work.
Thur	What is Floppy trying to say? Suggest speech bubbles for Floppy. Teacher scribes.	Practise sight recognition of key words for Stage 3.	**Group C** As above T	**Group D** As above T	**Group E** As above I	**Group A** As above I	**Group B** As above OA	**Group A** Read sentences. Read Floppy's speech bubbles.
Fri	Read story including Floppy's words. Use expression.	Practise/revise this week's high frequency words or spelling patterns.	**Group B** As above T	**Group C** As above T	**Group D** As above I	**Group E** As above I	**Group A** As above OA	**Group E** Read sentences. Check punctuation.

Fitting in with the National Literacy Framework

Word work: W10 to recognize common features of words, e.g. common spelling patterns; **W7** to read on sight high frequency words specific to graded books matched to ability.

Sentence work: S8 to begin using full stops to demarcate sentences.

Text work: T15 to make simple lists for reminding; **T3** to notice the difference between spoken and written forms through retelling stories.

T = Teacher   **I = Independent**   **OA = Other adult**

These weekly plans are intended as exemplars only and teachers will want to exercise their own skill and judgement when planning for the Literacy Hour.

Stage 3   By the Stream   Year 1 Term 1

Shared reading and writing

Monday: Predict the story from the cover and the pictures. Read the extended story. Use questions to help the children to predict the text. Read the text together.

Tuesday: Read story together, noticing full stops and using appropriate expression. Point to words as the children read. Find these key words: *couldn't, get, Get*. Use Context Cards to practise reading them.

Wednesday: Children take turns to read a page. Remind them what to do when you meet a new word. (Use the picture, look at the sound at the beginning of the word, look for spelling patterns you know, reread the whole sentence.)

Thursday: Shared writing: Decide what the other characters are saying. Write on speech bubbles. Children help with spellings.

Friday: Read the story together. One group acts out the story.

Word work

Awareness of critical features of words, such as length; revise use of capital letters.

Monday: Cover one word in the text on each page. Ask children to predict the word, using the length of the word as a clue. Write the word and check that you are right. Remember that names need capital letters.

Tuesday: Cover the first word in each sentence. Remember that the word identified will start with a capital letter whether it is a name or not.

Wednesday: Look for the longest and shortest words on each page. Count the letters in each.

Thursday: Make a list of words with two-, three-, and four-letters from the text and from words children know.

Friday: Practise reading, writing, and spelling this week's high frequency words and spelling patterns.

Guided group tasks (reading or writing)

Reading: Talk about the cover and the pictures. Predict the story in own words. Children read independently. Praise children for responding to full stops.

Writing: Assess children's ability to sound and name each letter of the alphabet in lower and upper case. You could use page 115 of *Group Activity Sheets Book 1*.

Independent activities

1: Listen to the story tape, talking stories, or use Stage 3 workbooks.

Group Activity Sheets Book 1: Use the notes on page 105 to introduce the following:

2: Word work (page 106) to recognize critical features of words, e.g. length.

3: Sentence work (page 107) to use a capital letter for 'I' and for the start of a sentence.

4: Text work (page 108) to write about events in personal experience linked to a variety of familiar incidents from stories.

5: Handwriting assessment (page 118) to form lower case letters in a form that will be easy to join later.

Plenary

Use this time to allow children to explain their work to others. It is also an opportunity to reinforce teaching points as they arise and to add to the morning's word work.

Suggested Weekly Plan — BY THE STREAM — STAGE 3 — YEAR 1 TERM 1

	Whole class – shared reading and writing.	Whole class – phonics, spelling, vocabulary, grammar.	Guided group tasks (reading or writing)	Guided group tasks (reading or writing)	Independent group tasks	Independent group tasks		Plenary
Mon	Predict story from title and cover. Read extended story and ask questions listed. Read text.	Cover first word in each sentence with post-its. Use length to help predict missing words, e.g. Kipper or He.	**Group A** Guided reading. Word length, GAS Bk1 p106. (T)	**Group B** Story tape, or workbook. Assess letter sounds and names GAS Bk1 115. (T)	**Group C** Write own version of story or use, GAS Bk1 p108. (I)	**Group D** Capital letters for I and the start of sentences, GAS Bk1 p107. (I)	**Group E** Assess handwriting, GAS Bk1 p118.	**Group A** Show and explain lists of words. **Group D** Read sentences.
Tues	Read story together, pointing to words as they are read. Find key words in story.	Cover first words as before. Ask children to tell you how to write missing words including capital letters.	**Group E** As above (T)	**Group A** As above (T)	**Group B** As above (I)	**Group C** As above (I)	**Group D** As above (OA)	**Group E** Show and explain lists of words. **Group B** Read stories.
Wed	Take turns to read a page. Remind children how to tackle a new word.	Find and list longest and shortest words on each page. Count the letters to reinforce length.	**Group D** As above (T)	**Group E** As above (T)	**Group A** As above (I)	**Group B** Word lotto Stage 4 or 5, Games Box 4–5. (I)	**Group C** As above (OA)	**Group D** Show and explain lists of words.
Thur	Write in speech bubbles to add what is being said.	List words with two, three or four letters from memory or from the text.	**Group C** As above (T)	**Group D** As above (T)	**Group E** As above (I)	**Group A** As above (I)	**Group B** As above (OA)	Read speech bubbles from story book.
Fri	Read the story together. Allocate roles and act the story.	Practise/revise this week's high frequency words or spelling patterns.	**Group B** As above (T)	**Group C** As above (T)	**Group D** As above (I)	**Group E** As above (I)	**Group A** As above (OA)	Another group of children act out the story.

Fitting in with the National Literacy Framework

Word work: W10 to recognize the critical features of words, e.g. length; **W2** to secure alphabetic letter knowledge; **W14** to form lower case letters correctly.

Sentence work: S9 to use a capital letter for 'I' and for the start of a sentence.

Text work: T9 to write about events in personal experience linked to incidents from stories; **T7** to re-enact stories through role play.

T = Teacher　　　**I = Independent**　　　**OA = Other adult**

These weekly plans are intended as exemplars only and teachers will want to exercise their own skill and judgement when planning for the Literacy Hour.

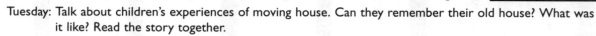

Stage 4   1 House for Sale   Year 1 Term 2

Shared reading and writing

Monday: Predict the story from the cover and the pictures. Read the extended story. Use the questions to help the children to predict the text. Read text together.

Tuesday: Talk about children's experiences of moving house. Can they remember their old house? What was it like? Read the story together.

Wednesday: Cover the new key words in the text: *for, like, house, this, room*. As you read the story ask children to predict the missing words. Practise reading these words on sight.

Thursday: Shared writing: Talk about Kipper. What did he do? Read the story again to find out. Suggest sentences about Kipper. Teacher scribes.

Friday: Enlarge an extract from the playscript for *House for Sale*. Discuss the different layout. Ask children to read part of the play.

Word work

Consolidate work on blending phonemes in CVC words; spell common words ending in *ff, ll, ss, ck, ng*.

Monday: Use the format shown on page 48 of *Group Activity Sheets Book 2* to link phonemes with mapping lines to generate CVC words.

Tuesday: Read and spell words ending with *ff* and *ll*. Change onsets to generate more words.

Wednesday: Read and spell words ending with *ss* and *ck*. Write lists.

Thursday: Read and spell words ending with *ng*. Change the vowel and the onset to generate more *ng* words.

Friday: Practise reading, writing, and spelling this week's high frequency words and spelling patterns.

Guided group tasks (reading or writing)

Reading: Talk about the cover and the pictures. Predict the story in own words. Read the story independently. Remind children about the variety of strategies to use when they meet new words.

Writing: Ask the children to make their own context cards for this story. Emphasise accuracy, neatness, and appropriate size writing for others to read.

Independent activities

1: Listen to the story tape, talking stories, or use Stage 4 workbooks.

Group Activity Sheets Book 2: Use the notes on page 11 to introduce the following:

2: Word work (page 12) to spell common words from Appendix List 1.

3: Sentence work (page 13) to predict text from the grammar, read on, leave a gap and reread.

4: Text work (page 14) to build simple profiles of characters from stories read.

5: Sequencing Cards for *House for Sale*. Ask the children to match the right sentences or write their own words to retell the story.

6: Use letters to make CVC words.

Plenary

Use this time to allow children to explain their work to others. It is also an opportunity to reinforce teaching points as they arise and to add to the morning's word work.

Suggested Weekly Plan — 1 HOUSE FOR SALE — STAGE 4 — YEAR 1 TERM 2

	Whole class – shared reading and writing.	Whole class – phonics, spelling, vocabulary, grammar.	Guided group tasks (reading or writing)	Guided group tasks (reading or writing)	Independent group tasks	Independent group tasks	Independent group tasks	Plenary
Mon	Introduce story through title, cover, and pictures. Predict story. Read extended story. Read text.	Revise blending phonemes in CVC words. Use GAS Bk 2 p48 to generate CVC words.	**Group A** Guided reading. Missing words, GAS Bk2 p12. (T)	**Group B** Story tape, talking story, or workbook. Guided reading or writing. (T)	**Group C** Missing verbs, GAS Bk 2 p13 or game from Games Box 4–5. (I)	**Group D** Use sequencing cards to retell story. Write own text. (I)	**Group E** All about Kipper, GAS Bk2 p14. (OA)	**Groups A and E** Show and explain their work.
Tues	Talk about children's experiences of moving to a new home. Read story.	Read and spell words ending with *ff, ll*. Change onsets of words to generate lists.	**Group E** As above or make CVC words with letters. (T)	**Group A** As above (T)	**Group B** As above (I)	**Group C** As above (I)	**Group D** As above (OA)	**Group C** Read own stories.
Wed	Cover new key words in story, ask children to predict. Practise reading them on sight.	Read and spell words ending in *ss, ck*. Write lists.	**Group D** As above (T)	**Group E** As above (T)	**Group A** As above (I)	**Group B** Word lotto Stage 4 or 5, Games Box 4–5. (I)	**Group C** As above (OA)	**Group D** Show missing words and check spellings.
Thur	Read story. Talk about Kipper. What did he do? What is he like? Teacher scribes. Children help with spellings.	Read and spell words ending with *ng*.	**Group C** As Group C (T)	**Group D** As above (T)	**Group E** As above (I)	**Group A** As above (I)	**Group B** As above (OA)	**Group B** Show their work about Kipper.
Fri	Playscript for *House for Sale*. Discuss how layout differs from story.	Practise/revise this week's high frequency words or spelling patterns.	**Group B** As above (T)	**Group C** As above (T)	**Group D** As above (I)	**Group E** As above or TG2 AS 4.13 half sentences. (I)	**Group A** As above (OA)	Another group reads the play to the class or acts out the story.

Fitting in with the National Literacy Framework

Word work: W9 to spell common words from Appendix List 1; **W2** to investigate, read and spell words ending in *ff, ll, ss, ck, ng*.

Sentence work: S3 to predict words from preceding words; **S5** to continue demarcating sentences in writing, ending a sentence with a full stop.

Text work: T15 to build simple profiles of characters; **T9** to become aware of character and dialogue; **T16** to use some of the elements of known stories to structure own writing.

T = Teacher   **I = Independent**   **OA = Other adult**

These weekly plans are intended as exemplars only and teachers will want to exercise their own skill and judgement when planning for the Literacy Hour.

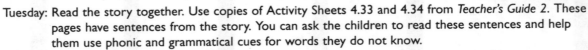

Stage 4   2 The New House   Year 1 Term 2

Shared reading and writing

Monday: Predict the story from the cover and the pictures. Read the extended story. Use the questions to help the children to predict the text. Read text together.

Tuesday: Read the story together. Use copies of Activity Sheets 4.33 and 4.34 from *Teacher's Guide 2*. These pages have sentences from the story. You can ask the children to read these sentences and help them use phonic and grammatical cues for words they do not know.

Wednesday: Read the story from the book, noticing punctuation and using appropriate expression. Find the key words in the story: *helped*, *big*, *things*, *man*. Practise reading them on sight.

Thursday: Shared writing: What happens when moving house? Ask children to tell you about their move or to tell what happens in story. Make a list of what happens – wrapping, filling boxes, unpacking etc.

Friday: Enlarge part of *The New House* playscript. Compare with story. Ask one group to read part of play.

Word work

Vocabulary extension; using grammatical cues; capital letters for names.

Monday: Look at the pictures and name objects being moved. Teacher writes the list. Add more things that have to be moved.

Tuesday: Read list of household objects. Use phonic cues to read them.

Wednesday: Use Activity Sheets 4.33 and 4.34 from *Teacher's Guide 2*. Ask children to find all the capital letters and mark them on the sheets. Talk about capital letters for names and for the beginning of sentences. Find examples of both in the classroom.

Thursday: Ask children to name cities, towns, and villages they know about. Make a list showing use of capital letters.

Friday: Practise reading, writing, and spelling this week's high frequency words and spelling patterns.

Guided group tasks (reading or writing)

Reading: Talk about the cover and the pictures. Predict the story in own words. Read the story independently. Show children how to read on past a new word then read the whole sentence again to help decode and make sense of an unknown word.

Writing: Help the children to use a picture dictionary to find out how to spell household items correctly.

Independent activities

1: Listen to the story tape, talking stories, or use Stage 4 workbooks.

Group Activity Sheets Book 2: Use the notes on page 15 to introduce the following:

2: Word work (page 16) to make collections of words related to particular topics.

3: Sentence work (page 17) to use capital letters for names.

4: Text work (page 18) to represent outlines of story plots using captions and pictures.

5: Cut up sentences from Activity Sheets 4.33 and 4.34 *Teacher's Guide 2* into individual words. Children have a sentence each and put the words in the right order.

6: Half sentences: Activity Sheet 4.14, explained on page 62 *Teacher's Guide 2*.

Plenary

Use this time to allow children to explain their work to others. It is also an opportunity to reinforce teaching points as they arise and to add to the morning's word work.

Suggested Weekly Plan — 2 THE NEW HOUSE — STAGE 4 — YEAR 1 TERM 2

	Whole class – shared reading and writing.	Whole class – phonics, spelling, vocabulary, grammar.	Guided group tasks (reading or writing)	Guided group tasks (reading or writing)	Independent group tasks			Plenary
Mon	Predict story from title and cover. Read extended story. Use questions to help children predict the text.	Vocabulary extension. List names of items shown being moved. Add more.	**Group A** Guided reading. Write captions, GAS Bk2 p18. — T	**Group B** Story tape, talking story, or workbook. Guided reading or writing. — T	**Group C** Sentence each from TG2 AS 4.33, 4.34. Cut up. Children put words in order. — I	**Group D** Capital letters for names, GAS Bk2 p17. — I	**Group E** Vocabulary, GAS Bk2 p16. Use picture dictionary for spellings. — OA	**Group E** Show words they have found in a dictionary.
Tues	Read story together. Read story from TG2 sheets 4.33 and 4.34 (no pictures).	Use phonics to read new words in list of household items.	**Group E** As above or half sentences, TG2 AS 4.14. — T	**Group A** As above — T	**Group B** As above — I	**Group C** As above — I	**Group D** As above — OA	**Group B** Explain sentences. **Group C** Show capital letters work.
Wed	Read story together paying attention to punctuation. Find the new key words in the story.	Find words with capital letters. Mark them on AS 4.33 and 4.34.	**Group D** As above — T	**Group E** As above — T	**Group A** As above — I	**Group B** Word lotto Stage 4 or 5, Games Box 4–5. — I	**Group C** As above — OA	**Group D** Show captions on van picture. Check spellings.
Thur	What happens when you move house? Children suggest events from experience. Teacher scribes.	List place names children mention or local places. Note capital letters. Make cities/ towns/villages word bank.	**Group C** As above — T	**Group D** As above — T	**Group E** As above — I	**Group A** As above — I	**Group B** As above — OA	**Group A** Show capital letters work.
Fri	Look at play script for *The New House.* Talk about layout. Read part of the play.	Practise/revise this week's high frequency words or spelling patterns.	**Group B** As above — T	**Group C** As above — T	**Group D** As above — I	**Group E** As above — I	**Group A** As above — OA	Another group reads the play or acts out the story.

Fitting in with the National Literacy Framework

Word work: W10 to make collections of words linked to particular topics.

Sentence work: S7 to use capital letters for names.

Text work: T14 to represent outlines for story plots; **T2** to assemble information from own experience; **T25** to use phonological, contextual, grammatical, and graphic knowledge to work out new words.

T = Teacher   **I = Independent**   **OA = Other adult**

These weekly plans are intended as exemplars only and teachers will want to exercise their own skill and judgement when planning for the Literacy Hour.

Stage 4   3 Come In!   Year I Term 2

3 Come In!
Roderick Hunt   Alex Brychta

Shared reading and writing

Monday: Predict the story from the cover and the pictures. Read the extended story. Use the questions to help the children to predict the text. Read text together.

Tuesday: Cover the number words. Read the story together. Predict the numbers from the pictures.

Wednesday: Take turns to read pages of the story. Cover words such as *children, biscuits, house*. Ask children to predict the missing words. Can they think of alternative words that might make sense? e.g. *friends* instead of *children*, *sweets* instead of *biscuits*.

Thursday: Shared writing: Why was Mum cross when she came back? What did she say to the children? What did they say to her? The teacher writes down the children's ideas.

Friday: Read the story together. Find new key words in the story: *came, Come, play, with, door*. Practise sight recognition of these words.

Word work

Adding *s* for plurals. Practise spelling number words.

Monday: Find and list words from the text that become plural by adding *s*. Refer to classroom labels for more examples, e.g. *pencils, rulers*.

Tuesday: Practise spelling the number words in the story. Extend to ten.

Wednesday: Put a number word with a noun, e.g. *two dogs*. Ask children to spell the words.

Thursday: Use pictures from the book to add more words that have *s* in the plural. Add to the list.

Friday: Practise reading, writing, and spelling this week's high frequency words and spelling patterns.

Guided group tasks (reading or writing)

Reading: Introduce the book. Talk about the story as a group. Scan the text for new words. Work out what they are. Read the story independently. Respond to any difficulties by sharing appropriate strategies.

Writing: Write a sensible sentence each, then change it to make a silly sentence. Talk about what is wrong with the silly sentences.

Independent activities

1: Listen to the story tape, talking stories, or use Stage 4 workbooks.

Group Activity Sheets Book 2: Use the notes on page 19 to introduce the following:

2: Word work (page 20) to read on sight number words to ten.

3: Sentence work (page 21) to expect text to make sense and to check for sense if it does not.

4: Text work (page 22) to retell stories, giving the main points in sequence.

5: Plurals: 'Lots of things' Activity Sheet 4.42 *Teacher's Guide 2*.

6: Half sentences: Activity Sheet 4.15 *Teacher's Guide 2*, explained on page 62.

Plenary

Use this time to allow children to explain their work to others. It is also an opportunity to reinforce teaching points as they arise and to add to the morning's word work.

Suggested Weekly Plan   3 COME IN!   STAGE 4   YEAR 1 TERM 2

	Whole class – shared reading and writing.	Whole class – phonics, spelling, vocabulary, grammar.	Guided group tasks (reading or writing)	Guided group tasks (reading or writing)	Independent group tasks			Plenary
Mon	Predict story from title and cover. Use questions to guide responses. Read extended story. Read text.	List words that have s for plurals, e.g. biscuit, television, door. Refer to class labels for more.	**Group A** Guided reading. Sentences, GAS Bk2 p21. — T	**Group B** Story tape, talking story, or workbook. Guided reading or writing. — T	**Group C** Number words, practise writing one to ten, GAS Bk2 p20. — I	**Group D** Plurals. Lots of things, TG2 AS 4.42	**Group E** Retell the story using GAS Bk2 p22.	**Group E** Read stories.
Tues	Read story together. Cover and predict number words.	Practise spelling number words. Extend to ten. Match words to figures.	**Group E** As above or half sentences, TG2 AS 4.15. — T	**Group A** As above — T	**Group B** As above — I	**Group C** As above	**Group D** As above — OA	**Group B** Show numbers, handwriting.
Wed	Take turns to read. Cover house, children, biscuits, television; predict missing words, suggest alternative.	Make up phrases that put a number with a noun that has s in the plural, e.g. two dogs. Practise spelling.	**Group D** As above — T	**Group E** As above — T	**Group A** As above — I	**Group B** Word lotto Stage 4 or 5, Games Box 4–5.	**Group C** As above — OA	**Group D** Read sentences and silly sentences. **Group C** Read stories.
Thur	Why was Mum cross? What did she say? What did the children say? Teacher scribes.	Use pictures (e.g. p10/11) to add to list of words with s for plurals.	**Group C** As above — T	**Group D** As above — T	**Group E** As above — I	**Group A** As above	**Group B** As above — OA	**Group A** Read plurals work. Add to list of s words.
Fri	Read the story. Find new key words in the story. Practise reading them.	Practise this week's high frequency words or spelling patterns.	**Group B** As above — T	**Group C** As above — T	**Group D** As above — I	**Group E** As above	**Group A** As above — OA	Read some of the best stories written this week.

Fitting in with the National Literacy Framework

Word work: W6 to read on sight high frequency words from Appendix List 1; **W8** to investigate and learn spellings of words with s for plurals.

Sentence work: S1 to expect text to make sense and check for sense if it doesn't; **S3** to predict words from preceding words and investigate sorts of words that fit, suggesting appropriate alternatives.

Text work: T4 to retell stories, giving main points in sequence; **T9** to become aware of character and dialogue.

T = Teacher   **I = Independent**   **OA = Other adult**

These weekly plans are intended as exemplars only and teachers will want to exercise their own skill and judgement when planning for the Literacy Hour.

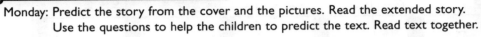

Stage 4 4 The Secret Room   Year 1 Term 2

Shared reading and writing

Monday: Predict the story from the cover and the pictures. Read the extended story. Use the questions to help the children to predict the text. Read text together.

Tuesday: Read the story together. Notice and respond to full stops. Find new key words in the story: *painted*, *found*, *opened*, *little*. Practise reading them.

Wednesday: Take turns to read. Use the pictures, the context and phonics to read new words. Practise sight recognition of key words.

Thursday: Shared writing: What else could have been under the sheet? A magic rocking horse? A sailing ship? Change the story from page 14 onwards. Discuss ideas, then the teacher scribes.

Friday: Read the story together to page 14 then read own version of the story. Ask the children which story they like best? The old one or the new one?

Word work

Recognize the critical features of words, e.g. length; revise *ch*, *sh*, *th*; spell words with initial consonant clusters.

Monday: Look carefully at words, noticing how the shape and length is often different. Draw some silhouettes to fit words or draw boxes that allow for ascenders and descenders. Predict words that will fit a given shape.

Tuesday: Revise words with *ch*, *sh*, *th* at the beginning or the end of words.

Wednesday: Think of words that start with *bl* and *br*; spell them.

Thursday: Think of words that start with *cl* and *cr*; spell them.

Friday: Practise reading, writing, and spelling this week's high frequency words and spelling patterns.

Guided group tasks (reading or writing)

Reading: Introduce the book. Talk about the story as a group. Scan the text for new words. Work out what they are. Read the story independently. Respond to any difficulties by sharing appropriate strategies.

Writing: Make up some questions about the story to ask the rest of the class. Practise expressing questions orally, then write down one question each.

Independent activities

1: Listen to the story tape, talking stories, or use Stage 4 workbooks.

Group Activity Sheets Book 2: Use the notes on page 23 to introduce the following:

2: Word work (page 24) to recognize the critical features of words, e.g. length.

3: Sentence work (page 25) to predict words from preceding words in sentences and investigate the sort of words that fit.

4: Text work (page 26) to present outlines of story plots using arrows to record the main incidents in order.

5: Choice of familiar books to read or games from Games Box for Stages 4–5.

Plenary

Use this time to allow children to explain their work to others. It is also an opportunity to reinforce teaching points as they arise and to add to the morning's word work.

Suggested Weekly Plan — YEAR 1 TERM 2 — STAGE 4 — 4 THE SECRET ROOM

Day	Whole class – shared reading and writing.	Whole class – phonics, spelling, vocabulary, grammar.	Guided group tasks (reading or writing)	Guided group tasks (reading or writing)	Independent group tasks			Plenary
Mon	Predict story from title and cover. Read extended story. Ask questions. Read text.	Look at words noticing the shape and length. Draw silhouettes or boxes to fit key words. Predict word to fit.	**Group A** Guided reading. Matching words to shapes, GAS Bk2 p24. — T	**Group B** Story tape, talking story, or workbook. Guided reading or writing. — T	**Group C** Completing sentences, GAS Bk2 p25. — I	**Group D** Read from choice of familiar books or game from Games Box 4–5. — I	**Group E** Use arrows to tell the story, GAS Bk2 p26. — OA	**Group A** Explain how they fitted words to their shapes. Draw some more word shapes.
Tues	Read story together. Notice and respond to full stops. Find new key words in the story.	Revise words with ch, sh, th as initial sound, as final sound.	**Group E** As above — T	**Group A** As above — T	**Group B** As above — I	**Group C** As above — I	**Group D** As above — OA	**Group E** Show words fitted to shape. Draw some more.
Wed	Take turns to read. Use pictures and phonics to work out new words. Sight recognition of key words.	Initial consonant blends: *bl* and *br*. List words; segment for spelling.	**Group D** As above — T	**Group E** As above — T	**Group A** As above — I	**Group B** Word lotto Stage 4 or 5, Games Box 4–5. — I	**Group C** As above — OA	**Group B** Explain game or talk about the book they chose.
Thur	What else could have been under the sheet? Change the story from page 14 onwards.	Initial consonant blends *cl* and *cr*; list words; segment for spelling.	**Group C** As above — T	**Group D** As above — T	**Group E** As above — I	**Group A** As above — I	**Group B** As above — OA	Read list of three letter words. **Group C** Read sentences.
Fri	Read the story together to page 14 then read new version written yesterday.	Practise/revise this week's high frequency words or spelling patterns.	**Group B** As above — T	**Group C** As above — T	**Group D** As above — I	**Group E** As above — I	**Group A** As above or write story of the secret room. — OA	Read class story. **Group D** Read sentences.

Fitting in with the National Literacy Framework

Word work: W7 to recognize the critical features of words, e.g. length; W3 to discriminate, read, and spell words with initial consonant clusters.

Sentence work: S3 to predict words from preceding words; S5 to continue demarcating sentences in writing, ending each sentence with a full stop.

Text work: T14 to represent the outlines of story plots using arrows. T16 to use some of the elements of known stories to structure own writing.

T = Teacher   I = Independent   OA = Other adult

These weekly plans are intended as exemplars only and teachers will want to exercise their own skill and judgement when planning for the Literacy Hour.

Stage 4   5 The Play   Year 1 Term 2

Shared reading and writing

Monday: Predict the story from the cover and the pictures. Read the extended story. Use the questions to help the children to predict the text. Read text together.

Tuesday: Read the story with expression. The children join in. Find new key words in the story: *There, outside, inside, her, him*.

Wednesday: Read text together. Talk about punctuation and how it affects the way we read. Read sentences to the children leaving a word out each time. Does it make sense? Can they make it make sense?

Thursday: Shared writing: Reread pages 14–17. Discuss who played which part. What do the children know about the story *The Wizard of Oz*? Write the story using children's suggestions and starting 'Once upon a time …'.

Friday: Read and add to the story of *The Wizard of Oz*. Use phonics for new words, e.g. *Emerald City*.

Word work

Reading and spelling words with initial consonant clusters.

Monday: Think of and spell words that start with *dr* and *dw*. Segment suggested words into phonemes for spelling.

Tuesday: Write any children's names that begin with consonant clusters. List words starting with *fl, fr*.

Wednesday: List words beginning with *gl, gr*. Segment words to hear each phoneme.

Thursday: Enlarge and use page 50 of *Group Activity Sheets Book 2*. This has phonemes to link with mapping lines to make words.

Friday: Practise reading, writing, and spelling this week's high frequency words and spelling patterns.

Guided group tasks (reading or writing)

Reading: Introduce the book. Talk about the story as a group. Scan the text for new words. Use a variety of cues to work out what they are. Read the story independently. Respond to any difficulties by discussing appropriate strategies.

Writing: Use any recent piece of writing. Help the child to improve content, spelling, or punctuation according to need.

Independent activities

1: Listen to the story tape, talking stories, or use Stage 4 workbooks.

Group Activity Sheets Book 2: Use the notes on page 27 to introduce the following:

2: Word work (page 28) to discriminate, read, and spell words with initial consonant clusters.

3: Sentence work (page 29) to use the term *sentence* appropriately.

4: Text work (page 30) to use some of the elements of known stories to structure own writing.

5: Choice of familiar books to read.

6: *Teacher's Guide 2:* Use Activity Sheet 4.2 for children to match the story characters to their parts in *The Wizard of Oz*.

Plenary

Use this time to allow children to explain their work to others. It is also an opportunity to reinforce teaching points as they arise and to add to the morning's word work.

Suggested Weekly Plan   5 THE PLAY   STAGE 4   YEAR I TERM 2

	Whole class – shared reading and writing.	Whole class – phonics, spelling, vocabulary, grammar.	Guided group tasks (reading or writing)	Guided group tasks (reading or writing)	Independent group tasks	Independent group tasks	Independent group tasks	Plenary
Mon	Talk about the title and cover. Look at pictures and predict story. Read extended story. Ask questions.	Initial consonant clusters: list words beginning with *dr, dw*. Segment words to spell.	**Group A** Guided reading. Consonant blends, GAS Bk2 p28. *(T)*	**Group B** Story tape, talking story, or workbook. Guided reading or writing. *(T)*	**Group C** Sentences, GAS Bk2 p29. *(I)*	**Group D** TG2 AS 4.2 or choice of familiar books.	**Group E** Write 'Wet playtime' story, GAS Bk2 p30. *(OA)*	**Group E** Read stories. Read word lists with consonant blends.
Tues	Read text with expression. Children join in. Find new key words in the story.	List children's names with initial consonant blends. List words starting with *fl, fr*.	**Group E** As above *(T)*	**Group A** As above *(T)*	**Group B** As above *(I)*	**Group C** As above	**Group D** As above *(OA)*	**Group B** Explain how they sorted out their sentences.
Wed	Read text together. Notice punctuation. Sensible sentences, listen and correct errors.	List words beginning with *gl, gr*. Segment words to hear each consonant clearly.	**Group D** As above *(T)*	**Group E** As above *(T)*	**Group A** As above *(I)*	**Group B** Word lotto Stage 4 or 5, Games Box 4–5.	**Group C** As above *(OA)*	**Group C** Read stories. Discuss any spellings they found difficult.
Thur	Write the story of *The Wizard of Oz* using children's knowledge of the story.	Consonant clusters Use GAS p50 to make words with mapping lines. List words made.	**Group C** As above *(T)*	**Group D** As above *(T)*	**Group E** As above *(I)*	**Group A** As above	**Group B** As above *(OA)*	**Group A** Show work or talk about books read.
Fri	Read and add to yesterday's story. Use phonics to work out new words.	Practise/revise this week's high frequency words or spelling patterns.	**Group B** As above *(T)*	**Group C** As above *(T)*	**Group D** As above *(I)*	**Group E** As above	**Group A** As above *(OA)*	**Group D** Show work. Read story of *The Wizard of Oz*.

Fitting in with the National Literacy Framework

Word work: W3 to discriminate read and spell words with initial consonant clusters.

Sentence work: S6 to use the term sentence appropriately.

Text work: T16 use elements of known stories to structure own writing; **T12** through shared writing to apply phonological, graphic knowledge, and sight vocabulary to spell words correctly.

T = Teacher   **I = Independent**   **OA = Other adult**

These weekly plans are intended as exemplars only and teachers will want to exercise their own skill and judgement when planning for the Literacy Hour.

Stage 4   6 The Storm   Year I Term 2

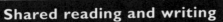

Shared reading and writing

Monday: Predict the story from the cover and the pictures. Read the extended story. Use the questions to help the children to predict the text. Read text together.

Tuesday: Read the story, responding to the punctuation. Find new key words in the story: *mended*, *storm*, *time*, *box*, *key*. Practise reading them.

Wednesday: Take turns to read the text with expression. Ask questions starting with 'why' so that children have to think of the reason, e.g. Why did the tree fall down?

Thursday: Ask children to retell the story in their own words. Reread the text to compare with oral version.

Friday: Shared writing: Show the children how to write a plan before writing a story. Use *The Storm* as a title. Ask the children to answer the questions: When was the storm? Who was caught in it? What happened to them? How did it end?

Word work

Revise words ending in *ff*, *ll*, *ss*, *ng*, *ck*. Practise sight recognition of Stage 4 key words.

Monday: Use *Biff*, *wall*, and *mess* to start lists of words ending with *ff*, *ll*, *ss*.

Tuesday: Use page 49 of *Group Activity Sheets Book 2* to generate more words ending with *ff*, *ll*, *ss*, *ng*, *ck* using mapping lines.

Wednesday: Read and spell words listed so far this week.

Thursday: Use Context Cards to practise sight recognition of Stage 4 key words.

Friday: Practise reading, writing, and spelling this week's high frequency words and spelling patterns.

Guided group tasks (reading or writing)

Reading: Introduce the book. Talk about the story as a group. Scan the text for new words. Use a variety of cues to work out what they are. Read the story independently. The teacher responds to any difficulties by discussing appropriate strategies.

Writing: Assess children's ability to spell words with initial consonant clusters by using some of these words in sentences for dictation.

Independent activities

1: Listen to the story tape, talking stories, or use Stage 4 workbooks.

Group Activity Sheets Book 2: Use the notes on page 31 to introduce the following:

2: Word work (page 32) to investigate, read, and spell words ending in *ff*, *ll*, *ss*, *ng*, *ck*.

3: Sentence work (page 33) to use capital letters for names.

4: Text work (page 34) to discuss reasons for, or causes of, incidents in stories.

5: Stage 4 key words assessment: If another adult is available he or she could assess Stage 4 key words using page 52 of *Group Activity Sheets Book 2*.

6: Games from Games Box for Stages 4 and 5.

Plenary

Use this time to allow children to explain their work to others. It is also an opportunity to reinforce teaching points as they arise and to add to the morning's word work.

Suggested Weekly Plan　　6 THE STORM　　STAGE 4　　YEAR I TERM 2

	Whole class – shared reading and writing.	Whole class – phonics, spelling, vocabulary, grammar.	Guided group tasks (reading or writing)	Guided group tasks (reading or writing)	Independent group tasks			Plenary
Mon	Predict story from title and cover. Read extended story and use questions. Read text.	Use *Biff*, *wall*, and *mess* to start lists of words with *ff*, *ll*, *ss* endings.	**Group A** Guided reading. Word endings, GAS Bk2 p32. (T)	**Group B** Story tape or workbook. Assess consonant blends. (T)	**Group C** Names, GAS Bk2 p33. (I)	**Group D** Reasons, GAS Bk2 p34. (I)	**Group E** Assess Stage 4 key words. (I)	**Group D** Read sentences.
Tues	Read text together. Notice punctuation. Point to words while reading. Find new key words in the story.	Use GAS p49 to make more words with *ck*, *ff*, *ng*, *ll*, *ss* endings using mapping lines.	**Group E** As above (T)	**Group A** As above (T)	**Group B** As above (I)	**Group C** As above (I)	**Group D** As above (I)	**Group C** Read sentences. OA
Wed	Take turns to read with expression. Ask questions to elicit reasons for events.	Read and spell words with *ck*, *ff*, *ll*, *ng*, *ss* endings. Add more to lists.	**Group D** As above (T)	**Group E** As above (T)	**Group A** As above (I)	**Group B** Word lotto Stage 4 or 5, Games Box 4–5. (I)	**Group C** As above (I)	**Group B** Read sentences. **Group A** Show and explain work. OA
Thur	Retell story in own words. Compare with written text. What else might have been found?	Use flash cards or GAS Bk2 p52 to practise sight recognition of all Stage 4 key words.	**Group C** As above (T)	**Group D** As above (T)	**Group E** As above (I)	**Group A** As above (I)	**Group B** As above (I)	Use *Treasure Hunt* clue cards (Games Box 4–5) to practise spelling. OA
Fri	Plan a story about a storm, When? Who? What? How did it end? Teacher scribes.	Practise/revise this week's high frequency words or spelling patterns.	**Group B** As above (T)	**Group C** As above (T)	**Group D** As above (I)	**Group E** As above or key words lotto, Games Box 4–5. (I)	**Group A** As above (I)	**Group E** Explain work. OA

Fitting in with the National Literacy Framework

Word work: W2 to investigate words ending in *ff*, *ll*, *ss*, *ck*, *ng*; **W3** to discriminate, read, and spell words with initial consonant clusters; **W11** ensure correct letter orientation, formation, and proportion.

Sentence work: S7 to use capital letters for names.

Text work: T7 to discuss reasons for and causes of incidents in stories; **T16** to use some elements of known stories to structure own writing.

OA = Other adult　　**I = Independent**　　**T = Teacher**

These weekly plans are intended as exemplars only and teachers will want to exercise their own skill and judgement when planning for the Literacy Hour.

Stage 5 1 The Magic Key Year 1 Term 3

Shared reading and writing

Monday: Predict the story from the cover and the pictures. Read the story using discussion pointers on page 125 *Teacher's Guide 2.*

Tuesday: Read story together, reacting to punctuation. Cover *glowing* in the text. Ask children to predict the word. What else would make sense? Find all other new key words: *picked, like, began, magic.*

Wednesday: Ask the children to retell the part of the story about the mouse. Reread that part of the text and compare with the oral version.

Thursday: Shared writing: Start from page 17 of the story but imagine that the door opened when Biff pushed it. What happened next? The children suggest ideas and the teacher writes the new story.

Friday: Ask different children to read to page 17 of story. Praise them for reading with expression and for responding to punctuation. Read changes to the story written yesterday.

Word work

Recognizing words by common spelling patterns.

Monday: Use words from the text, change the onset to get new words, e.g. *box, fox; bed, red, fed; got, hot, lot,* etc. Remind children that rhymes help us to spell.

Tuesday: Segment high frequency words from Appendix List 1 into phonemes to spell them, e.g. *but, did, dig, got, had, has, him, his, not, off.*

Wednesday: Look for words inside words, e.g. *win, in, do,* in *window; lip* in *slippers, pen* in *pencil.*

Thursday: Segment and spell more words from the high frequency list, e.g. *from, just, much, must, next, than, that, them, then, will, with.*

Friday: Practise reading, writing, and spelling this week's high frequency words and spelling patterns.

Guided group tasks (reading or writing)

Reading: Introduce the book. Talk about the story as a group. Scan the text for new words. Use a variety of cues to work out what they are. Read the story independently. Talk about the magic and what happens.

Writing: Ask each child to write a sentence, then to read it leaving one word out. Ask the other children to correct the sentence by putting in a word that makes sense. Help the children to recognize when a sentence sounds right and when it makes sense.

Independent activities

1: Use Stage 5 workbooks or read playscripts at Stages 4 and 5.

Group Activity Sheets Book 2: Use the notes on page 53 to introduce the following:

2: Word work (page 54) to recognize words by common spelling patterns.

3: Sentence work (page 55) to expect reading to make sense and to check for sense if it does not.

4: Text work (page 56) to write about significant incidents from known stories.

5: Use rhyming card games from Rhyme and Analogy Card Games.

Plenary

Use this time to allow children to explain their work to others. It is also an opportunity to reinforce teaching points as they arise and to add to the morning's word work.

Suggested Weekly Plan

I THE MAGIC KEY · STAGE 5 · YEAR I TERM 3

	Whole class – shared reading and writing.	Whole class – phonics, spelling, vocabulary, grammar.	Guided group tasks (reading or writing)	Guided group tasks (reading or writing)	Independent group tasks	Independent group tasks	Independent group tasks	Plenary
Mon	Use the title, cover, and pictures to predict story. Read the story using discussion pointers (TG2 p125).	Use words from text, change onset to make new words, e.g. box, fox. Make a list.	**Group A** Guided reading Sentences, GAS Bk2 p55. — T	**Group B** Workbook or Stage 4 or 5 playscripts. Guided reading or writing. — T	**Group C** Rhyme and Analogy Card Game (rhyming words). — I	**Group D** Rhyming words, GAS Bk2 p54. — I	**Group E** Write story of Biff, Chip and the mouse, GAS Bk2 p56. — OA	**Group E** Read own stories. Spelling game, e.g. *Treasure Hunt* clue cards (Games Box 4–5).
Tues	Read together, with expression, notice punctuation. Cover *glowing*. What would fit instead?	Segment high frequency words into phonemes and spell them.	**Group E** As above or make own sentences (TG2 AS 5.14). — T	**Group A** As above — T	**Group B** As above — I	**Group C** As above — I	**Group D** As above — OA	**Group C** Read rhyming words. Spelling game.
Wed	Ask children to retell part of the story about the mouse. Compare with the text.	Look for words inside words, e.g *win*, *in*, *do* in *window*.	**Group D** As above — T	**Group E** As above — T	**Group A** As above — I	**Group B** Word lotto Stage 4 or 5, Games Box 4–5. — I	**Group C** As above — OA	**Group D** Read sentences. Spelling game.
Thur	Suppose door opens when children push it, what happens? Teacher scribes.	Segment and spell more words from the high frequency list.	**Group C** As above — T	**Group D** As above — T	**Group E** As above — I	**Group A** As above — I	**Group B** As above — OA	**Group B** Read stories. **Group A** Read rhyming words.
Fri	Take turns to read the story to page 17. Read new ending to story.	Practise/revise this week's high frequency words or spelling patterns.	**Group B** As above — T	**Group C** As above — T	**Group D** As above — I	**Group E** As above — I	**Group A** As above — OA	Read class story. Practise high frequency words.

Fitting in with the National Literacy Framework

Word work: W5 to recognize words by common spelling patterns; W1 to segment words into phonemes for spelling.

Sentence work: S1 to expect reading to make sense and check if it does not; S2 to use awareness of grammar to predict text.

Text work: T13 to write about significant incidents from known stories; T12 to apply phonological, graphic knowledge, and sight vocabulary to spell words accurately.

T = Teacher   **I = Independent**   **OA = Other adult**

These weekly plans are intended as exemplars only and teachers will want to exercise their own skill and judgement when planning for the Literacy Hour.

Stage 5   2 Pirate Adventure   Year 1 Term 3

Shared reading and writing

Monday: Predict the story from the cover and the pictures. Read the story using discussion pointers on page 126 Teacher's Guide 2.

Tuesday: Read the story together, responding to the punctuation. Discuss 'an adventure'. When do we use 'an' for 'a'? Find several examples.

Wednesday: Take turns to read, pointing to the words and responding to punctuation. Find new key words in the story: *don't, Don't, help, an, adventure.*

Thursday: Shared writing: Make up questions about the story or pictures. Teacher writes the questions and class answers them. Are the questions clear? Do they need changing to be clearly understood?

Friday: Retell the story together, deciding which are the most important points. Practise the new key words.

Word work

Vowels and consonants.

Monday: Explain which letters are vowels, and which are consonants. Ask the children to name the vowels in words in the text; name the consonants in those words.

Tuesday: Ask the children to scan the text on a page of the story to find words with given numbers of vowels or consonants, e.g. 'Find a word with two vowels.'

Wednesday: Ask the children to think of a word with a given number of vowels and consonants, e.g.'Tell me a word that has two consonants and one vowel.'

Thursday: Ask the children to suggest four vowels and four consonants. Write them on a board and ask them to make words using those letters.

Friday: Practise reading, writing, and spelling this week's high frequency words and spelling patterns.

Guided group tasks (reading or writing)

Reading: Introduce the book. Talk about the story as a group. Scan the text for new words. Use a variety of cues to work out what they are. Read the story independently. Find two events that are important parts of the story (e.g. A pirate came up). Find two events that are not so important (e.g. Wilf picked up a shell).

Writing: Ask the children to make up some questions about the story. Show them how to write questions, using question marks.

Independent activities

1: Use Stage 5 workbooks or read playscripts at Stages 4 and 5.

Group Activity Sheets Book 2: Use the notes on page 57 to introduce the following:

2: Word work (page 58) to know the terms *vowel* and *consonant*.

3: Sentence work (page 59) to reinforce knowledge of the term *sentence*.

4: Text work (page 60) to recognize an ordered sequence of events, using words like *first, then, next*.

5: Games from Games Box for Stages 4–5.

Plenary

Use this time to allow children to explain their work to others. It is also an opportunity to reinforce teaching points as they arise and to add to the morning's word work.

Suggested Weekly Plan   2 PIRATE ADVENTURE   STAGE 5   YEAR 1 TERM 3

	Whole class – shared reading and writing.	Whole class – phonics, spelling, vocabulary, grammar.	Guided group tasks (reading or writing)	Guided group tasks (reading or writing)	Independent group tasks			Plenary
Mon	Predict story from title, cover, and pictures. Read the story using discussion pointers, TG2 p126.	Explain vowels and consonants. Find the vowels in some words. Name the consonants in words.	**Group A** Guided reading. Vowels/consonants, GAS Bk2 p58. — T	**Group B** Workbook or read playscripts. Guided reading or writing. — T	**Group C** Answering questions, GAS Bk2 p59. — I	**Group D** Spelling tree game or lotto game from Games Box 4–5. — I	**Group E** Ordering events, GAS Bk2 p60. — I	'How many vowels in …?' game. Use high frequency words, e.g. *said, like*.
Tues	Read the story together. Notice punctuation and use expression. When to use 'an'.	Find words in the text with given numbers of vowels or consonants.	**Group E** As above — T	**Group A** As above — T	**Group B** As above — I	**Group C** As above — I	**Group D** As above — OA	**Groups D and E** Show and explain work.
Wed	Take turns to read pages of the story. Point to words and notice punctuation. New key words.	Think of words with given number of vowels/consonants, e.g. two consonants, one vowel.	**Group D** As above — T	**Group E** As above — T	**Group A** As above — I	**Group B** Word lotto Stage 4 or 5, Games Box 4–5. — I	**Group C** As above — OA	**Groups A and C** Show and explain work.
Thur	Use the pictures to make up questions, e.g. on page 13 "Who is up a tree?" Teacher scribes.	Suggest four consonants and four vowels. How many words can you make?	**Group C** As above — T	**Group D** As above — T	**Group E** As above — I	**Group A** As above — I	**Group B** As above — OA	**Group B** Show work. Play vowel and consonant game.
Fri	Retell the story together. Separate main points from less important ones.	Practise/revise this week's high frequency words or spelling patterns.	**Group B** As above — T	**Group C** As above — T	**Group D** As above — I	**Group E** As above — I	**Group A** As above — OA	Read retelling of story. Check punctuation.

Fitting in with the National Literacy Framework

Word work: W9 to know the terms *vowel* and *consonant*; **W1** to segment words into phonemes for spelling.

Sentence work: S6 to reinforce knowledge of the term *sentence*; **S7** to add question marks to questions.

Text work: T18 to recognize an ordered sequence of events using words like *first, then, next*; **T5** to retell stories; to give the main points in sequence, and to pick out significant incidents.

T = Teacher   **I = Independent**   **OA = Other adult**

These weekly plans are intended as exemplars only and teachers will want to exercise their own skill and judgement when planning for the Literacy Hour.

Stage 5   3 The Dragon Tree   Year 1 Term 3

Shared reading and writing

Monday: Predict the story from the cover and the pictures. Read the story using discussion pointers on page 127 *Teacher's Guide 2*.

Tuesday: Read the story together, responding to the punctuation. Find new key words in the story: *about, frightened, away, from, called, took.*

Wednesday: Take turns to read, pointing to the words and responding to punctuation. Practise reading new key words in sentences and alone.

Thursday: Shared writing: Floppy's escape. Use wording on page 16 to begin this part of story. Ask children to retell what happened next in own words. Help the children keep to a consistent narrative style.

Friday: Talk about Floppy's escape. Who was brave? Who had good ideas? Who was frightened? Reread the story written yesterday.

Word work

Spelling patterns for long e and long *a* phonemes.

Monday: Use *tree, key,* and *read* to start lists of words with long e phonemes. Decide which spelling pattern to use for each word suggested.

Tuesday: Read lists of words written yesterday. Add some more. Which spelling pattern is used most often? Put words with e phonemes into sentences.

Wednesday: Use *came, tail,* and *away* to start lists of words with different spelling patterns for the long *a* phoneme.

Thursday: Read and spell the words listed yesterday; add more words to each list. Which spelling pattern is the most common?

Friday: Practise reading, writing, and spelling this week's high frequency words and spelling patterns.

Guided group tasks (reading or writing)

Reading: Introduce the book. Talk about the story as a group. Scan text for new words. Use variety of cues to work out what they are. Read story independently. Choose words such as *called* and *nasty*. Which words could be used instead? Ask children to think of other words that could be changed without changing story.

Writing: Review any recent piece of written work, helping the children to improve content, punctuation, spelling, or presentation according to need.

Independent activities

1: Use Stage 5 workbooks or read playscripts from Stages 4 and 5.

Group Activity Sheets Book 2: Use the notes on page 61 to introduce the following:

2: Word work (page 62) to know common spelling patterns for the long vowel phoneme ee and ai.

3: Sentence work (page 63) to predict words from previous text.

4: Text work (page 64) to use labelled diagrams to show 'What we know about ...'

5: *Teacher's Guide 2*: Use the 'Sort them out' activity using Activity Sheet 5.12 or games from Games Box for Stages 4–5.

Plenary

Use this time to allow children to explain their work to others. It is also an opportunity to reinforce teaching points as they arise and to add to the morning's word work.

Suggested Weekly Plan — 3 THE DRAGON TREE — STAGE 5 — YEAR 1 TERM 3

	Whole class – shared reading and writing.	Whole class – phonics, spelling, vocabulary, grammar.	Guided group tasks (reading or writing)	Guided group tasks (reading or writing)	Independent group tasks	Independent group tasks	Independent group tasks	Plenary
Mon	Predict story from title, cover, and pictures. Read the story using discussion pointers, TG2 p127.	Find words in text with long e phonemes: *tree, read, key*. Think of more and make lists.	**Group A** Guided reading. Long e phonemes, GAS Bk2 p62.	**Group B** Workbook or read playscripts. Guided reading or writing.	**Group C** Missing words, GAS Bk2 p63.	**Group D** 'Sort them out' activity, TG2 AS 5.12 or Games Box 4–5.	**Group E** 'All about dragons' poster, GAS Bk2 p64.	Read long e word lists. Add some more words. Make a list for *she, he* etc.
Tues	Read the story together. Notice punctuation and use expression. Find new key words.	Revise long e phonemes. Which spelling is most frequently used?	**Group E** As above	**Group A** As above	**Group B** As above	**Group C** As above	**Group D** As above	**Group E** Show phonemes work. Read lists and add more words.
Wed	Take turns to read pages of the story. Point to words and notice punctuation. Practise new key words.	Use *came, tail, away* to begin lists with long *a* phoneme.	**Group D** As above	**Group E** As above	**Group A** As above	**Group B** Word lotto Stage 4 or 5, Games Box 4–5.	**Group C** As above	**Groups C and A** Show and explain work.
Thur	Retell the part of the story telling how Floppy escaped. Teacher scribes.	Practise spelling words with long *a* phonemes. Add more to the list.	**Group C** As above	**Group D** As above	**Group E** As above	**Group A** As above	**Group B** As above	**Group B** Show posters. Practise long e words spellings.
Fri	Talk about Floppy's escape. Who had good ideas? Who was frightened?	Practise/revise this week's high frequency words or spelling patterns.	**Group B** As above	**Group C** As above	**Group D** As above	**Group E** As above	**Group A** As above	**Group D** Show missing words work.

T = Teacher   I = Independent   OA = Other adult

Fitting in with the National Literacy Framework

Word work: W1 spelling patterns for the long phonemes *ee* and *ai*.

Sentence work: S4 to predict words from previous text, grouping a range of words that might 'fit'.

Text work: T21 to use labelled drawings to show 'What we know about ...'; T13 to write about significant incidents from stories.

These weekly plans are intended as exemplars only and teachers will want to exercise their own skill and judgement when planning for the Literacy Hour.

Stage 5   4 Gran   Year 1 Term 3

Shared reading and writing

Monday: Predict the story from the cover and the pictures. Read the story using discussion pointers on page 128 *Teacher's Guide 2.*

Tuesday: Read the story together, responding to the punctuation. Find new key words in the story: *It's, everyone, go, Go, my, out.*

Wednesday: Take turns to read, pointing to the words and responding to punctuation. Notice capital letters in the story and in the illustrations.

Thursday: Shared writing: What did the children tell Mum? What did Mum say to Gran? Write the conversation.

Friday: Reread the story. Read the conversation written yesterday. Talk about Gran. What is she like as a person. Would you like her? Do you have a gran like her?

Word work

Verb endings *ing* and *ed*. Regular patterns. Mention common irregular patters.

Monday: Read *play, playing, played* and talk about changed endings. Make up a sentence for each word to explain the use of each version. Predict and spell the endings for *jump, climb, want.*

Tuesday: Cover verbs in the story that have regular patterns for *ing* and *ed*. Ask the children to predict and spell the missing words.

Wednesday: Look at common verbs ending in *e*, e.g. *like, take, make*. What happens when we add *ing*? Spell the words.

Thursday: Use *room, tune, flew,* and *blue* to list words with the long *oo* phoneme. Practise spelling the words.

Friday: Practise reading, writing, and spelling this week's high frequency words and spelling patterns.

Guided group tasks (reading or writing)

Reading: Introduce the book. Talk about the story as a group. Read the story independently. Find and read all the notices that use capital letters. Discuss the use of capital letters. Ask the children to think of other notices they have seen that use capitals, e.g. road names.

Writing: Read some 'blurbs' from story books. Ask the children to write a 'blurb' for the book they are currently reading. This can be an individual or a group task.

Independent activities

1: Stage 5 workbooks or choose from familiar books.

Group Activity Sheets Book 2: Use the notes on page 65 to introduce the following:

2: Word work (page 66) to investigate and learn spellings of verbs with *ed* (past tense) and *ing* (present tense) endings.

3: Sentence work (page 67) for other common uses of capitalization.

4: Text work (page 68) to use the title, cover page, pictures, and 'blurbs' to predict the content of familiar stories.

5: Read *Gran* playscripts.

6: Games from Games Box for Stages 4–5.

Plenary

Use this time to allow children to explain their work to others. It is also an opportunity to reinforce teaching points as they arise and to add to the morning's word work.

Suggested Weekly Plan   4 GRAN   STAGE 5   YEAR I TERM 3

	Whole class – shared reading and writing.	Whole class – phonics, spelling, vocabulary, grammar.	Guided group tasks (reading or writing)	Guided group tasks (reading or writing)	Independent group tasks	Independent group tasks	Independent group tasks	Plenary
Mon	Predict story from title, cover, and pictures. Read the story using discussion pointers, TG2 p128.	Notice how verbs change endings, e.g. play, plays, playing, played. Predict and write endings for jump, climb, want.	**Group A** Guided reading. Correct verbs, GAS Bk2 p66. [T]	**Group B** Workbook or read familiar books. Guided reading or writing. [T]	**Group C** Capital letters for notices, GAS Bk2 p67. [I]	**Group D** Choice of games from Games Box 4–5 or playscript. [I]	**Group E** A book cover about Gran, GAS Bk2 p68. [OA]	**Group E** Show book covers. **Group A** Show verb work.
Tues	Read the story together. Notice punctuation and use expression. Find key words.	Cover verbs in the text that match a regular pattern. Spell them.	**Group E** As above [T]	**Group A** As above [T]	**Group B** As above [I]	**Group C** As above [I]	**Group D** As above [OA]	**Group B** Show capital letters work. **Group C** Show covers.
Wed	Take turns to read pages of the story. Point to words and notice punctuation. Look for capital letters in story.	Look for verbs with e at the end. What happens when you add ing?	**Group D** As above [T]	**Group E** As above [T]	**Group A** As above [I]	**Group B** Word lotto Stage 4 or 5, Games Box 4–5. [I]	**Group C** As above [OA]	**Group D** Show work. How do take, say, and make change?
Thur	What did the children tell Mum? What did Mum say? Write the conversation.	*Use room, tune, flew, blue to start lists of words with the long oo phoneme.*	**Group C** As above [T]	**Group D** As above [T]	**Group E** As above [I]	**Group A** As above [I]	**Group B** As above [OA]	Practise changing regular verbs by adding ing and ed.
Fri	Reread the story, including the conversation written yesterday. Talk about Gran.	Practise/revise this week's high frequency words or spelling patterns.	**Group B** As above [T]	**Group C** As above [T]	**Group D** As above [I]	**Group E** As above [I]	**Group A** As above [OA]	Look at and discuss the most interesting book covers.

Fitting in with the National Literacy Framework

Word work: W6 to investigate and learn spelling of verbs with ed and ing endings; **W1** the common spelling patterns for long oo phoneme.

Sentence work: S5 other common uses of capitalization; **S7** to add question marks to questions.

Text work: T7 to use title, cover, and 'blurbs' to predict content of stories; **T12** to apply phonological, graphic knowledge, and sight vocabulary to spell words accurately.

T = Teacher   **I = Independent**   **OA = Other adult**

These weekly plans are intended as exemplars only and teachers will want to exercise their own skill and judgement when planning for the Literacy Hour.

Stage 5   5 Castle Adventure   Year 1 Term 3

Shared reading and writing

Monday: Predict the story from the cover and the pictures. Read the story using discussion pointers on page 129 *Teacher's Guide 2*.

Tuesday: Read the story together, responding to the punctuation. Look for the new key words in the story: *of*, *Help*, *turned*, *into*, *One*. Practise reading them.

Wednesday: Take turns to read, pointing to the words and responding to punctuation. Practise making up questions to ask each other, e.g. What colour was Gran's jumper? What was on the witch's tray?

Thursday: Shared writing: All about witches. Use Activity Sheet 5.4 from *Teacher's Guide 2*. Use knowledge of other stories to make generalized statements about witches. The teacher writes down the children's ideas.

Friday: Retell, then reread the story. Look at and discuss other stories that have witches in them.

Word work

Read and spell common words for colours (Appendix List 1).

Monday: Scan text of the story for colour words. Add more colour words. Segment them into phonemes for spelling.

Tuesday: Practise 'look, say, cover, spell' method for learning how to spell common colour words.

Wednesday: Add more words to the list of colours, e.g. by finding names of colours on paints, coloured pencils, shade cards. Make a list for vocabulary extension.

Thursday: Practise spelling common colour words, segment into phonemes to spell accurately; blend phonemes to reread more unusual words on colour list, e.g. *burnt umber*.

Friday: Practise reading, writing, and spelling this week's high frequency words and spelling patterns, including colour words.

Guided group tasks (reading or writing)

Reading: Introduce the book. Talk about the story as a group. Scan the text for new words. Use a variety of cues to work out what they are. The children read the story independently. Take turns to ask each other questions about the text.

Writing: Think of words that describe the three witches. Make a list of adjectives. Decide which words sound best.

Independent activities

1: Use Stage 5 workbooks or choose from familiar books.

Group Activity Sheets Book 2: Use the notes on page 69 to introduce the following:

2: Word work (page 70) to read on sight common colour words.

3: Sentence work (page 71) to add question marks to questions.

4: Text work (page 72) to compose carefully selected sentences.

5: Games from Games Box for Stages 4–5.

6: Read *Castle Adventure* playscript.

Plenary

Use this time to allow children to explain their work to others. It is also an opportunity to reinforce teaching points as they arise and to add to the morning's word work.

Suggested Weekly Plan | 5 CASTLE ADVENTURE | STAGE 5 | YEAR 1 TERM 3

	Whole class – shared reading and writing.	Whole class – phonics, spelling, vocabulary, grammar.	Guided group tasks (reading or writing)	Guided group tasks (reading or writing)	Independent group tasks			Plenary
Mon	Predict story from title, cover, and pictures. Read story using discussion pointers, TG2 p129.	Collect colour words from text. List more colours. Segment into phonemes for spelling.	**Group A** Guided reading. Colour words, GAS Bk2 p70. *T*	**Group B** Workbooks or familiar books. Guided reading or writing. *T*	**Group C** Questions and answers, GAS Bk2 p71. *I*	**Group D** Games from Games Box 4–5 or playscript. *I*	**Group E** Writing a spell, GAS Bk2 p72. *OA*	Spelling colour words. **Group A** Show their work and spell some colour words.
Tues	Read the story together. Notice punctuation and use expression. Find key words.	Practise reading and spelling common colour words.	**Group E** As above *T*	**Group A** As above *T*	**Group B** As above *I*	**Group C** As above *I*	**Group D** As above *OA*	**Group D** Read spells. Draw attention to choice of words.
Wed	Take turns to read pages of the story. Point to words and notice punctuation. Make up questions.	Add more to list of colours, e.g. by looking at colour names on crayons, pencils, and paints.	**Group D** As above *T*	**Group E** As above *T*	**Group A** As above *I*	**Group B** Word lotto Stage 4 or 5, Games Box 4–5. *I*	**Group C** As above *OA*	**Group C** Read spells. Draw attention to choice of words.
Thur	Use AS 5.4 TG2 All about witches. Children suggest ideas and spelling., Teacher scribes.	Revise and spell colour words. Segment into phonemes if necessary.	**Group C** As above *T*	**Group D** As above *T*	**Group E** As above *I*	**Group A** As above *I*	**Group B** As above *OA*	**Group E** Show questions and answers work. Read witches poster.
Fri	Recall story and retell in own words. Talk about other stories with witches.	Practise/revise this week's high frequency words including colour words.	**Group B** As above *T*	**Group C** As above *T*	**Group D** As above *I*	**Group E** As above *I*	**Group A** As above *OA*	**Group B** Read colours. Add more to class list if possible.

Fitting in with the National Literacy Framework

Word work: W4 to read on sight common words (colours) from Appendix List 1; W1 to segment words into phonemes for spelling; W8 collect words linked to particular topics.

Sentence work: S7 to add question marks to questions.

Text work: T16 to compose carefully selected sentences; T21 use captions for pictures to show 'What we know about …'.

T = Teacher   I = Independent   OA = Other adult

These weekly plans are intended as exemplars only and teachers will want to exercise their own skill and judgement when planning for the Literacy Hour.

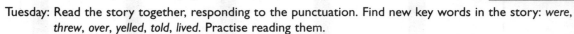

Stage 5   6 Village in the Snow   Year 1 Term 3

Shared reading and writing

Monday: Predict the story from the cover and the pictures. Read the story using discussion pointers on page 130 *Teacher's Guide 2*.

Tuesday: Read the story together, responding to the punctuation. Find new key words in the story: *were, threw, over, yelled, told, lived*. Practise reading them.

Wednesday: Retell the main points of story, then read it again. Compare oral and written versions. Which points are important? Which points are less important?

Thursday: Shared writing: Enlarge a story written this week by in individual activity time. Praise the good things. Discuss 'better' words that could have been used, e.g. instead of *said*, instead of *cross*.

Friday: Read story. Where is it set? Which country could it be? Use pictures in non-fiction books to find similar landscapes.

Word work

Read and spell words with long *o* and long *ie* phonemes.

Monday: Use *snow, coat, home*, and *go* to start lists of words with those spelling patterns and long *o* phoneme.

Tuesday: Read and practise spelling words listed yesterday. Add some more.

Wednesday: Use *lie, like, fight*, and *fly* to start lists of spelling patterns for words with a long *i* phoneme.

Thursday: Read and spell yesterday's list. Add more words.

Friday: Practise reading, writing, and spelling this week's high frequency words and spelling patterns.

Guided group tasks (reading or writing)

Reading: Introduce the book. Talk about the story as a group. Scan the text for new words. Use a variety of cues to work out what they are. The children read the story independently. Ask the children to find important and less important events in the story.

Writing: Assess sentence writing. You could use page 90 from *Group Activity Sheets Book 2*. This asks the children to write sensible sentences using a given vocabulary.

Independent activities

1: Use Stage 5 workbooks or read familiar books.

Group Activity Sheets Book 2: Use the notes on page 73 to introduce the following:

2: Word work (page 74) to know the common spelling patterns for the long phonemes *oa* as in *boat*.

3: Sentence work (page 75) to predict text from the grammar.

4: Text work (page 76) to retell stories, to give the main points in sequence, and to pick out significant incidents.

5: If another adult is available you could use page 86 of the *Group Activity Sheets Book 2* to assess children's ability to build words with long vowel phonemes. For independent work use *Village in the Snow* playscripts.

Plenary

Use this time to allow children to explain their work to others. It is also an opportunity to reinforce teaching points as they arise and to add to the morning's word work.

Suggested Weekly Plan   6 VILLAGE IN THE SNOW   STAGE 5   YEAR 1 TERM 3

	Whole class – shared reading and writing.	Whole class – phonics, spelling, vocabulary, grammar.	Guided group tasks (reading or writing)	Guided group tasks (reading or writing)	Independent group tasks			Plenary
Mon	Predict story from title, cover, and pictures. Read the story using discussion pointers, TG2 p130.	Look for words with long *o* phonemes in the text, e.g *snow*, *coat*, *home*, *go*. Add more to each list.	**Group A** Guided reading. Long *o* phonemes, GAS Bk2 p74. — T	**Group B** Workbook or read familiar books. Assess sentence writing, GAS Bk2 p90. — T	**Group C** Choose a word to fill the gap, GAS Bk2 p75. — I	**Group D** Story writing, GAS Bk2 p76. — I	**Group E** Assess long vowel spellings, GAS Bk2 p86. — OA	**Group A** Explain work with phonemes. Everyone reads lists.
Tues	Read the story together. Notice punctuation and use expression. Find key words.	Read long *o* word lists. Use onset and rime to generate more words.	**Group E** As above — T	**Group A** As above — T	**Group B** As above — I	**Group C** As above — I	**Group D** As above — OA	**Group C** Read stories. Notice use of punctuation.
Wed	Retell then reread the story. Compare oral story with the text. Which points are important?	Use *like*, *lie*, *fight*, and *fly* to make lists of word with the long *i* phoneme.	**Group D** As above — T	**Group E** As above — T	**Group A** As above — I	**Group B** Word lotto Stage 4 or 5, Games Box 4–5. — I	**Group C** As above — OA	**Group B** Read stories. Notice use of punctuation.
Thur	Read one of the children's stories. Praise all the good things, suggest an improvement.	Read lists with long *i* phoneme. Add some more words.	**Group C** As above — T	**Group D** As above — T	**Group E** As above — I	**Group A** As above — I	**Group B** As above — OA	**Group D** Read sentences.
Fri	Read the story together. Where is this story set? Which country could it be?	Practise/revise this week's high frequency words or spelling patterns.	**Group B** As above — T	**Group C** As above — T	**Group D** As above — I	**Group E** As above — I	**Group A** As above — OA	**Group E** Read stories.

Fitting in with the National Literacy Framework

Word work: W1 common spelling patterns for *oa* as in *boat*, *ie* as in *lie*; **W1** the common spelling patterns for each long vowel phoneme.

Sentence work: S2 predict text from grammar; **S6** through reading and writing to reinforce the term *sentence*; **S3** to read familiar texts aloud with pace and expression appropriate to grammar.

Text work: T5 to retell stories, giving the main points in sequence; **T12** to apply phonological, graphic knowledge, and sight vocabulary to spell words accurately.

T = Teacher   I = Independent   OA = Other adult

These weekly plans are intended as exemplars only and teachers will want to exercise their own skill and judgement when planning for the Literacy Hour.

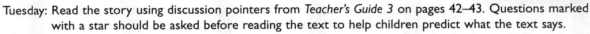
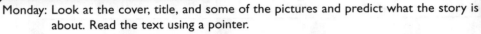

Stage 6   In the Garden   Year 2 Term 1

Shared reading and writing

Monday: Look at the cover, title, and some of the pictures and predict what the story is about. Read the text using a pointer.

Tuesday: Read the story using discussion pointers from *Teacher's Guide 3* on pages 42–43. Questions marked with a star should be asked before reading the text to help children predict what the text says.

Wednesday: Read the story together. Use punctuation to read with expression. Use general discussion points on page 43 to encourage the children to express ideas and opinions.

Thursday: Shared writing: Imagine being very small in the playground. What would steps and plants look like? Teacher scribes children's ideas for similes.

Friday: Read the story together. Read the comparisons made yesterday. Which ones do you like the best?

Word work

Revising long vowel phonemes in simple words.

Monday: Ask children to suggest words with a long *ai* phoneme, e.g. *rain, day, came*. Revise spelling patterns for the sound and list further suggestions.

Tuesday: List words with long ee phoneme, e.g. *feet, bean*.

Wednesday: List words with long ie phoneme, e.g *sky, high, tie, time*.

Thursday: List words with long oe and ue phonemes, e.g. *home, low, coat, blue, flew, soon, tune*.

Friday: Practise spelling or reading high frequency words or spelling patterns learned this week.

Guided group tasks (reading or writing)

Reading: Look at cover and pictures to talk about the story. Remind children to use the pictures and phonics if they find a new word. Listen as children read aloud at their own speed. Use any difficulties to remind children of useful strategies.

Writing: Draw children's attention to similes, e.g. 'The grass was like a jungle'. Make up some more similes, e.g. 'The bee was like a ...'. Write down at least one simile each, using the pictures in the book for ideas.

Independent activities

1: Use Stage 6 workbooks or read familiar books.

Group Activity Sheets Book 3: Use the notes on page 15 to introduce the following:

2: Word work (page 16) to revise spelling patterns for long vowel digraphs.

3: Sentence work (page 17) to use awareness of grammar to decipher new words.

4: Text work (page 18) to understand time and sequential relationships in stories.

5: *Teacher's Guide 3*: What was it like? activity introduced on page 78 and using Activity Sheet 14.

Plenary

Use this time to allow children to explain their work to others. It is also an opportunity to reinforce teaching points as they arise and to add to the morning's word work.

Suggested Weekly Plan   IN THE GARDEN   STAGE 6   YEAR 2 TERM 1

	Whole class – shared reading and writing	Whole class – phonics, spelling, vocabulary, grammar	Guided group tasks (reading or writing)	Guided group tasks (reading or writing)	Independent group tasks			Plenary
Mon	Predict story from title, cover, and pictures. Read the story to the children.	Revise spelling patterns for long *ai* phoneme. Children spell words, teacher lists them.	**Group A** Guided reading. Long vowels, GAS Bk3 p16. (T)	**Group B** Workbooks or choice of familiar books. Guided reading or writing. (T)	**Group C** Missing words, GAS Bk3 p17. (I)	**Group D** What was it like? TG3 Owls AS 14. (I)	**Group E** GAS Bk3 p18 ordering sentences. Check work. (OA)	**Group A** Show long vowels work. Read lists from word work.
Tues	Read the story together. Use discussion pointers, TG3 p42–43.	Revise spelling patterns for long *ee* phoneme. Spell and list words.	**Group E** As above (T)	**Group A** As above (T)	**Group B** As above (I)	**Group C** As above (I)	**Group D** As above (OA)	**Group E** Show long vowels work.
Wed	Read the story together. Point to words and notice punctuation. Use general discussion, TG3 p43.	Revise spelling patterns for long *ie* phoneme. Spell and list words.	**Group D** As above (T)	**Group E** As above (T)	**Group A** As above (I)	**Group B** Word lotto Stage 4 or 5, Games Box 4–5. (I)	**Group C** As above (OA)	**Group C** Explain how they ordered the sentences to retell the story.
Thur	Imagine being very small in the playground. What would it look like? Teacher scribes.	Revise spelling patterns for long *oe* and *ue* phonemes. Spell and list words.	**Group C** As above (T)	**Group D** As above (T)	**Group E** As above (I)	**Group A** As above (I)	**Group B** As above (OA)	**Group B** Read sentences in order.
Fri	Read the story. Read the ideas for similes written yesterday.	Practise/revise this week's high frequency words or spelling patterns.	**Group B** As above (T)	**Group C** As above (T)	**Group D** As above (I)	**Group E** As above (I)	**Group A** As above (OA)	**Group D** Show and explain missing words work.

Fitting in with the National Literacy Framework

Word work: W1 to secure identification, spelling, and reading of long vowel digraphs in simple words.

Sentence work: S1 to use awareness of grammar to decipher new or unfamiliar words; **S4** to reread their own writing for sense and punctuation.

Text work: T4 to understand time and sequential relationships in stories. **T10** to use story structure to write about own experience in similar form.

T = Teacher   **I = Independent**   **OA = Other adult**

These weekly plans are intended as exemplars only and teachers will want to exercise their own skill and judgement when planning for the Literacy Hour.

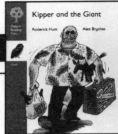

Stage 6   Kipper and the Giant   Year 2 Term 1

Shared reading and writing

Monday: Look at the cover, title, and some of the pictures and predict what the story is about. Read the text using a pointer.

Tuesday: Read the story using the starred questions from the discussion pointers in *Teacher's Guide 3* on pages 45–46 to help children predict the text.

Wednesday: Read the story together, pointing to the words. Use punctuation to read with expression. Use general discussion points on page 46 *Teacher's Guide 3* to encourage children to express thoughts and opinions.

Thursday: Act out the meeting between Kipper and the Giant.

Friday: Shared writing: Reread pages 18–21. Show children how to write the conversation between Kipper and the Giant as a playscript.

Word work

Common spelling patterns for the vowel phonemes *oo* (as in *book*), *ar*, *oy*, *ow*.

Monday: Introduce the spelling patterns used for the phoneme *ou* in *house*, e.g. *now*, *shouted*. Write lists with *ou* and *ow* spelling patterns

Tuesday: Introduce the spelling patterns for the phoneme *oy* in *boy* and *pointed*. Use words children suggest to make lists with each spelling pattern.

Wednesday: Introduce *ar* phoneme in *party*. Ask children to suggest more words. Encourage them to suggest the spelling for the whole word, e.g. *car*, *far*, *smart*, *start*.

Thursday: Introduce the spelling patterns for the phoneme *oo* in *book* and *u* in *put*. Ask children to suggest and spell more words with each pattern.

Friday: Practise spelling or reading high frequency words or spelling patterns learned this week.

Guided group tasks (reading or writing)

Reading: Look at cover and pictures to talk about the story. Show children how to read ahead leaving a gap for a new word, using the rest of the sentence as a clue. Listen as children read aloud. Note any difficulties. Praise strategies that children use.

Writing: Ask the children 'why?' questions about the story. Ask each child to write an answer to a question using 'because' in the sentence.

Independent activities

1: Use Stage 6 workbooks or read familiar books.

Group Activity Sheets Book 3: Use the notes on page 19 to introduce the following:

2: Word work (page 20) looking for words with the same sound and spelling pattern.

3: Sentence work (page 21) using words and phrases that link sentences from selection provided. If an adult is available to be with this group the children would benefit from discussion when choosing the best word.

4: Text work (page 22) choosing the reason for an event in the story from alternatives provided.

5: *Teacher's Guide 3*: 'If I were a friendly giant' activity. A short piece of writing and illustration explained on page 75 and using Activity Sheet 1.

Plenary

Use this time to allow children to explain their work to others. It is also an opportunity to reinforce teaching points as they arise and to add to the morning's word work.

Suggested Weekly Plan   KIPPER AND THE GIANT   STAGE 6   YEAR 2 TERM 1

	Whole class – shared reading and writing.	Whole class – phonics, spelling, vocabulary, grammar.	Guided group tasks (reading or writing)	Guided group tasks (reading or writing)	Independent group tasks	Independent group tasks	Independent group tasks	Plenary
Mon	Predict story from title, cover, and pictures. Read the story.	Spelling patterns ow and ou. Use house, shouted, and now to start lists of words with this phoneme.	**Group A** Guided reading. Spelling patterns, GAS Bk3 p20. — T	**Group B** Workbook or read familiar book. Guided reading. — T	**Group C** Answering questions, GAS Bk3 p22. — I	**Group D** If I were a friendly giant, TG3 Owls AS 1. — I	**Group E** Discuss words that link sentences, GAS Bk3 p21. — OA	**Group A** Explain spelling patterns work. Read lists from word work.
Tues	Read the story together. Use discussion pointers, TG3 p45–46.	Spelling patterns oy and oi. Use boy and pointed to start lists. Add lists to word banks.	**Group E** As above — T	**Group A** As above — T	**Group B** As above — I	**Group C** As above — I	**Group D** As above — OA	**Group C** Read stories. **Group D** Read sentences.
Wed	Read the story together. Point to words and notice punctuation. Use general discussion, TG3 p46.	Spelling pattern ar. Use party to start list. Change beginning and end to find more words.	**Group D** As above — T	**Group E** As above — T	**Group A** As above — I	**Group B** Word lotto Stage 4 or 5, Games Box 4–5. — I	**Group C** As above — OA	**Group B** Explain questions and answers work.
Thur	Act out the part of the story when the giant comes back. What does the giant say? What does Kipper say?	Spelling pattern oo as in book and u in put. Add more words. Display and use all word lists as word banks.	**Group C** As above — T	**Group D** As above — T	**Group E** As above — I	**Group A** As above — I	**Group B** As above — OA	**Group E** Read questions and answers. Reread word lists if time.
Fri	Recall dialogue between the giant and Kipper. Write as a play script.	Practise/revise this week's high frequency words or spelling patterns.	**Group B** As above — T	**Group C** As above — T	**Group D** As above — I	**Group E** As above — I	**Group A** As above — OA	Take turns to read dialogue between Kipper and the Giant.

Fitting in with the National Literacy Framework

Word work: W3 the common spelling patterns for the vowel phonemes oo (as in good), ar, oy, ow.

Sentence work: S2 to find examples of words and phrases that link sentences; **S3** to recognize and take account of commas and exclamation marks in reading aloud with proper expression.

Text work: T5 to identify and discuss reasons for events in stories, linked to plot; **T9** to apply phonological, graphic knowledge, and sight vocabulary to spell words accurately.

T = Teacher   I = Independent   OA = Other adult

These weekly plans are intended as exemplars only and teachers will want to exercise their own skill and judgement when planning for the Literacy Hour.

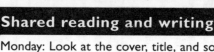

Stage 6   The Outing   Year 2 Term 1

Shared reading and writing

Monday: Look at the cover, title, and some of the pictures and predict what the story is about. Read the text using a pointer.

Tuesday: Read story using discussion pointers from pages 47–48 *Teacher's Guide 3* to help children to predict text. Read the story.

Wednesday: Read story together. Point out exclamation marks and commas. Notice how they affect expression. Use general discussion ideas on page 48 to encourage children to express own ideas and opinions.

Thursday: Shared writing: Talk about any class outing. Teacher writes simple report from children's memories. Children contribute to spellings.

Friday: Retell part of the story, e.g. How Wilf lost his shoe. Reread that part of the story and compare with oral version.

Word work

Words that have the same sound, but different spellings.

Monday: Start with different spellings for children's names: *Clare, Claire; Steven, Stephen.* List other common words, such as *pear, pair.*

Tuesday: Add to the list, asking the children 'Is there another way to spell ...', e.g. another way to spell 'bean'?

Wednesday: Cover *to, too, know, see, here* in the text. Ask children to spell them correctly. What is the alternative spelling and meaning?

Thursday: Make up sentences using each spelling of common words. Use as a display.

Friday: Practise spelling or reading high frequency words or spelling patterns learned this week.

Guided group tasks (reading or writing)

Reading: Talk about the story using the cover, title and illustrations to predict what happens. Read independently. Reread pages 6–11 noticing and responding to exclamation marks and commas in the text.

Writing: Discuss then write sentences to show correct spellings of *their* and *there*.

Independent activities

1: Use Stage 6 workbooks or read familiar books.

Group Activity Sheets Book 3: Use the notes on page 23 to introduce the following:

2: Word work (page 24) with words with the same sounds but different spellings.

3: Sentence work (page 25) to recognize and take account of commas and exclamation marks when reading aloud.

4: Text work (page 26) to use story structure to write about own experience in same/similar form.

5: *Teacher's Guide 3*: Activity Sheet 8 'What happened next?' Children write the last event in a sequence from the story.

Plenary

Use this time to allow children to explain their work to others. It is also an opportunity to reinforce teaching points as they arise and to add to the morning's word work.

Suggested Weekly Plan — THE OUTING — STAGE 6 — YEAR 2 TERM 1

Day	Whole class – shared reading and writing.	Whole class – phonics, spelling, vocabulary, grammar.	Guided group tasks (reading or writing)	Guided group tasks (reading or writing)	Independent group tasks	Independent group tasks	Independent group tasks	Plenary
Mon	Predict story from title, cover, and pictures. Read the story.	Words with same sound but different spellings. Start with children's names, e.g. Clare, Claire.	**Group A** Guided reading. Punctuation, GAS Bk3 p25. (T)	**Group B** Workbook or read familiar book. Guided reading. (T)	**Group C** Write about an outing, GAS Bk3 p26. (I)	**Group D** What happened next? TG3 Owls AS 8. (I)	**Group E** Same sound, different spellings, GAS Bk3 p24.	**Group E** Explain words with same sound but different spellings.
Tues	Read the story together. Use discussion pointers, TG3 p47–48.	More words with same sound but different spelling, e.g. here, hear, to, two, too.	**Group E** As above (T)	**Group A** As above (T)	**Group B** As above (I)	**Group C** As above (I)	**Group D** As above (OA)	**Group C** Read 'What happened next.'
Wed	Read the story. Notice commas and exclamation marks. Use general discussion, TG3 p48.	Cover to, too, know, rain, see, here. Children choose correct spelling.	**Group D** As above (T)	**Group E** As above (T)	**Group A** As above (I)	**Group B** Word lotto Stage 4 or 5, Games Box 4–5. (I)	**Group C** As above (OA)	**Group A** Read retelling of story or account of an outing.
Thur	Recall any class event or outing and list main points. Teacher scribes.	Make up sentences to show which spelling of a word to use.	**Group C** As above (T)	**Group D** As above (T)	**Group E** As above (I)	**Group A** As above (I)	**Group B** As above (OA)	**Group B** Talk about words with same sound, different spelling.
Fri	Retell one incident from the story. Compare oral and text versions.	Practise/revise this week's high frequency words.	**Group B** As above (T)	**Group C** As above (T)	**Group D** As above (I)	**Group E** As above (I)	**Group A** As above (OA)	**Group D** Read own stories or accounts.

Fitting in with the National Literacy Framework

Word work: W4 to investigate and classify words with the same sounds but different spellings.

Sentence work: S3 to recognize and take account of commas and exclamation marks in reading aloud.

Text work: T10 to use story structure to write about own experience in same/similar form; **T3** to be aware of difference between spoken and written language by comparing oral recounts with the text.

T = Teacher   I = Independent   OA = Other adult

These weekly plans are intended as exemplars only and teachers will want to exercise their own skill and judgement when planning for the Literacy Hour.

Stage 6   Land of the Dinosaurs   Year 2 Term I

Shared reading and writing

Monday: Look at the cover, title, and some of the pictures and predict what the story is about. Read the text using a pointer.

Tuesday: Read the story using discussion pointers from pages 49–50 *Teacher's Guide 3*.

Wednesday: Read the story together with pace and expression. Remind children how to use the pictures, grammar, and phonics to read new words. Use general discussion points on page 50 *Teacher's Guide 3*.

Thursday: Shared writing: Talk about the setting of the story. Plan a story set in the time of the dinosaurs. How would it start? Who would be in it? What would happen to them?

Friday: Retell the story from memory. How did Biff feel when she found out there was no film in the camera. What did she say?

Word work

Add s to nouns for plurals; Verbs with *ing* and *ed*.

Monday: Add s to nouns for plurals using classroom items as examples.

Tuesday: Scan the text for words ending in s. Which ones are plurals? How can you tell?

Wednesday: Start with playing and played. Ask children for suggestions to add to each list. Practise spelling words suggested.

Thursday: Scan the text for verbs ending in *ing* and *ed*. Add them to yesterday's lists.

Friday: Practise spelling or reading high frequency words or spelling patterns learned this week.

Guided group tasks (reading or writing)

Reading: Talk about the story using the cover, title, and illustrations to predict what happens. Read the story independently. Draw attention to children reading with good expression.

Writing: Reread any recent piece of writing and check that it makes sense and that the punctuation is correct.

Independent activities

1: Use Stage 6 workbooks or read familiar books.

Group Activity Sheets Book 3: Use the notes on page 27 to introduce the following:

2: Word work (page 28) using word endings s, *ed* and *ing* to support their reading and spelling.

3: Sentence work (page 29) to reread own writing for sense and punctuation.

4: Text work (page 30) to use language of time to structure a sequence of events.

5: Retell the story and write what happened next using Owls Activity Sheet 9 from *Teacher's Guide 3*. There is space for the children to complete each sentence using the words given and to add one more sentence, e.g. The magic took the childen to the land *of the dinosaurs. 'I don't want this adventure'* said *Nadim*. Alternative activity – read a playscript.

Plenary

Use this time to allow children to explain their work to others. It is also an opportunity to reinforce teaching points as they arise and to add to the morning's word work.

Suggested Weekly Plan — LAND OF THE DINOSAURS STAGE 6 — YEAR 2 TERM 1

	Whole class – shared reading and writing	Whole class – phonics, spelling, vocabulary, grammar	Guided group tasks (reading or writing)	Guided group tasks (reading or writing)	Independent group tasks	Independent group tasks	Independent group tasks	Plenary
Mon	Predict story from title, cover, and pictures. Read the story to the children.	Add s to nouns for plurals. Find examples in classroom labels.	**Group A** Guided reading. Writing sentences. GAS Bk3 p29. — T	**Group B** Workbook or read familiar book. Guided reading. — T	**Group C** ing and ed endings, GAS Bk3 p28. — I	**Group D** Retell the story, TG3 Owls AS9 or playscript. — I	**Group E** Linking words, GAS Bk3 p30.	**Group C** Explain ing and ed words work. — OA
Tues	Read the story together. Use discussion pointers, TG3 p49–50.	Find words in the text ending in s. Are they all plurals?	**Group E** As above — T	**Group A** As above — T	**Group B** As above — I	**Group C** As above — I	**Group D** As above	**Group D** Read story with linking words in place. Discuss use of linking words. — OA
Wed	Read the story. Use phonics, grammar, and the pictures to decipher new words. Use general discussion, TG3 p50.	Children suggest ing words, write and add ed version, e.g. playing; played.	**Group D** As above — T	**Group E** As above — T	**Group A** As above — I	**Group B** Word lotto Stage 4 or 5, Games Box 4–5. — I	**Group C** As above	**Group A** Talk about ing and ed words. Add more words that fit the pattern. — OA
Thur	Talk about the setting of the story. Plan own 'Land of the dinosaurs' story.	Scan the text for words ending ing or ed. Make lists. Change one to the other if possible.	**Group C** As above — T	**Group D** As above — T	**Group E** As above — I	**Group A** As above — I	**Group B** As above	**Group E** Show ing and ed work. — OA
Fri	Retell the story from memory. What did Biff feel like at the end?	Practise/revise this week's high frequency words.	**Group B** As above — T	**Group C** As above — T	**Group D** As above — I	**Group E** As above — I	**Group A** As above	**Group B** Read sentences. — OA

Fitting in with the National Literacy Framework

Word work: W7 to use word endings s, ed, ing to support their reading and spelling.

Sentence work: S4 to reread own writing for sense and punctuation.

Text work: T11 to use language of time to structure a sequence of events; **T9** to apply phonological, graphic knowledge, and sight vocabulary to spell words accurately.

T = Teacher   **OA = Other adult**   **I = Independent**

These weekly plans are intended as exemplars only and teachers will want to exercise their own skill and judgement when planning for the Literacy Hour.

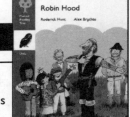

Stage 6   Robin Hood   Year 2 Term 1

Shared reading and writing

Monday: Look at the cover, title, and some of the pictures and predict what the story is about. Read the text using a pointer.

Tuesday: Read the story using discussion pointers from pages 51–53 *Teacher's Guide 3* to help the children to predict the text.

Wednesday: Read story together, noticing and responding to commas, exclamation marks, and question marks. Use general discussion points on page 52 to get children to express their own ideas and opinions.

Thursday: Shared writing: Make a list of characters in the Robin Hood play for the programme. Use capital letters correctly for names.

Friday: Read children's own instructions on how to rescue Robin Hood already written this week. Check that the sequence makes sense.

Word work

Vocabulary extension; practise sight recognition of key words and high frequency words.

Monday: Use *recorder* and *guitar* to start a class list of musical instruments. Ask the children for other suggestions; use phonemes to work out spellings.

Tuesday: Use other books, including reference books, to find more instruments. Add them to the list.

Wednesday: Practise sight recognition of words at Stage 6. These are listed in *Group Activity Sheets Book 3* page 40.

Thursday: Revise, read, and spell words from Appendix List 1.

Friday: Practise spelling or reading high frequency words or spelling patterns learned this week.

Guided group tasks (reading or writing)

Reading: Talk about the story using the cover, title, and illustrations to predict what happens. Read the story independently. Respond to commas, exclamation marks, and question marks by reading with appropriate expression.

Writing: Discuss how best to use capital letters to make a poster for the Robin Hood pantomime. Contribute to a group poster giving appropriate information.

Independent activities

1: Use Stage 6 workbooks or read familiar books.

Group Activity Sheets Book 3: Use the notes on page 31 to introduce the following:

2: Word work (page 32) to practise handwriting joins.

3: Sentence work (page 33) to revise knowledge about the other uses of capitalization.

4: Text work (page 34) to write simple instructions.

5: Retell the story and write what happened next using Owls Activity Sheet 10 from *Teacher's Guide 3*. There is space for the children to complete each sentence using the words given and to add one more sentence, e.g. The magic took the children to *a wood. It was the wood where Robin Hood lived.* Alternative activity – read a playscript.

Plenary

Use this time to allow children to explain their work to others. It is also an opportunity to reinforce teaching points as they arise and to add to the morning's word work.

Suggested Weekly Plan　　ROBIN HOOD　　STAGE 6　　YEAR 2 TERM 1

	Whole class – shared reading and writing.	Whole class – phonics, spelling, vocabulary, grammar.	Guided group tasks (reading or writing)	Guided group tasks (reading or writing)	Independent group tasks			Plenary
Mon	Predict story from title, cover, and pictures. Read the story.	Vocabulary extension. Start with *recorder* and *guitar* and add more instruments to list.	**Group A** Guided reading. Capital letters, Gas Bk3 p33. — T	**Group B** Workbook or read familiar book. Guided reading. — T	**Group C** Writing instructions, GAS Bk3 p34. — I	**Group D** Retell the story, TG3 Owls AS10 or playscript. — I	**Group E** Practise handwriting joins, GAS Bk3 p32. — OA	**Group E** Show and handwriting. **Group C** Explain and read instructions.
Tues	Read the story together. Use discussion pointers, TG3 p51–53.	Recall other stories with instruments. Add to list. Children suggest spellings.	**Group E** As above — T	**Group A** As above — T	**Group B** As above — I	**Group C** As above — I	**Group D** As above — OA	**Group B** Explain and read instructions for setting Robin free.
Wed	Read story together. Notice commas, question and exclamation marks. Use discussion points, TG3 p52.	Practise sight recognition of words at Stage 6, GAS Bk3 p40.	**Group D** As above — T	**Group E** As above — T	**Group A** As above — I	**Group B** Word lotto Stage 4 or 5, Games Box 4–5. — I	**Group C** As above — OA	**Group D** Show capital letters work. Check correct letter formation.
Thur	Write a list of characters for the programme. Use capital letters correctly for names.	Revise, read, and spell words from Appendix List 1.	**Group C** As above — T	**Group D** As above — T	**Group E** As above — I	**Group A** As above — I	**Group B** As above — OA	**Group A** Read playscript or explain game.
Fri	How to rescue Robin. Instructions. Use children's work, GAS Bk3 p34.	Practise/revise this week's high frequency words.	**Group B** As above — T	**Group C** As above — T	**Group D** As above — I	**Group E** As above — I	**Group A** As above — OA	Read list of instructions. Add more if necessary.

Fitting in with the National Literacy Framework

Word work: W11 to practise handwriting patterns; W12 to begin using and practising the four basic handwriting joins; W5 to read on sight and spell 30 more words from Appendix List 1.

Sentence work: S5 to revise other uses of capitalization and use in writing; S3 to recognize and take account of comma and exclamation marks when reading aloud with appropriate expression.

Text work: T15 to write simple instructions; T18 to use appropriate register in writing instructions.

T = Teacher	I = Independent	OA = Other adult

These weekly plans are intended as exemplars only and teachers will want to exercise their own skill and judgement when planning for the Literacy Hour.

Stage 6   The Treasure Chest   Year 2 Term 1

Shared reading and writing

Monday: Look at the cover, title, and some of the pictures and predict what the story is about. Read the text using a pointer.

Tuesday: Read the story using discussion pointers from pages 54–56 *Teacher's Guide 3*.

Wednesday: Read the story together with pace and expression. Use the general discussion points on page 56 *Teacher's Guide 3* to encourage the children to express their own ideas and opinions.

Thursday: Read pages 1–7 about the swimming test. Ask the children to bring any swimming certificates they have to school. Read these.

Friday: Write a poem about going swimming using *ing* words. An example is on page 80 *Teacher's Guide 3*.

Word work

Revise vowels and consonants.

Monday: Remind the children which letters are vowels and which are consonants. Ask them to think of words with a given number of each, e.g. two vowels, two consonants.

Tuesday: Choose words from the text or high frequency words and ask the children how many vowels or how many consonants are in particular words. Practise spelling CVC words.

Wednesday: Think of words to match given patterns of vowels and consonants.

Thursday: Make up vowel/consonant games, e.g. think of a word with a vowel in the middle.

Friday: Practise spelling or reading high frequency words or spelling patterns learned this week.

Guided group tasks (reading or writing)

Reading: Assess reading from *The Treasure Chest* without picture cues. Use text extract on page 44 *Group Activity Sheets Book 3*. Mark any difficulties to assess child's needs.

Writing: Look at a recent piece of each child's handwriting. Consider improvements together. Ask the children to copy a sentence or two from the book in their best handwriting.

Independent activities

1: Use Stage 6 workbooks or read familiar books.

Group Activity Sheets Book 3: Use the notes on page 35 to introduce the following:

2: Word work (page 36) to secure understanding and use of the terms *vowel* and *consonant*.

3: Sentence work (page 37) to use simple organizational devices to indicate sequences and relationships.

4: Text work (page 38) to use appropriate register in writing instructions.

5: Retell the story and write what happened next using Owls Activity Sheet 11 from *Teacher's Guide 3*. There is space for the children to complete each sentence using the words given and to add one more sentence, e.g. The children had masks and flippers *and tanks of air. They could swim under water.*

Plenary

Use this time to allow children to explain their work to others. It is also an opportunity to reinforce teaching points as they arise and to add to the morning's word work.

Suggested Weekly Plan THE TREASURE CHEST STAGE 6 YEAR 2 TERM 1

	Whole class – shared reading and writing.	Whole class – phonics, spelling, vocabulary, grammar.	Guided group tasks (reading or writing)	Guided group tasks (reading or writing)	Independent group tasks	Independent group tasks	Independent group tasks	Plenary
Mon	Predict story from title, cover, and pictures. Read the story.	Revise vowels and consonants. Make words with any two vowels and any two consonants.	**Group A** Guided reading. Vowels and consonants, GAS Bk3 p36. **T**	**Group B** Workbook or read familiar book. Assess reading, GAS Bk3 p44. **T**	**Group C** Ordering sentences, GAS Bk3 p37. **I**	**Group D** Retell the story, TG3 Owls AS11. **I**	**Group E** Write swimming certificate, GAS Bk3 p38. **OA**	**Group A** Explain how vowels and consonants work. Make more words, e.g. CVVC.
Tues	Read the story together. Use discussion pointers, TG3 p54–56.	Find vowels in a series of words. Find consonants in a series of words. Make CVC words.	**Group E** As above **T**	**Group A** As above **T**	**Group B** As above **I**	**Group C** As above **I**	**Group D** As above **OA**	**Group E** Explain vowels and consonants work.
Wed	Read the story together with pace and expression. Use general discussion, TG3 p56.	Think of words to fit given patterns of vowels and consonants, e.g. CVCC, CVCV.	**Group D** As above **T**	**Group E** As above **T**	**Group A** As above **I**	**Group B** Word lotto Stage 4 or 5, Games Box Stage 4–5. **I**	**Group C** As above **OA**	**Group C** Read swimming certificates.
Thur	Read pages 1–7 about swimming test. Read real swimming certificates.	Make up vowel/consonant games: think of words with given numbers of either.	**Group C** As above **T**	**Group D** As above **T**	**Group E** As above **I**	**Group A** As above **I**	**Group B** As above **OA**	**Group B** Read swimming certificates.
Fri	Write a poem about going swimming using ing words, see TG3 p80.	Practise/revise this week's high frequency words.	**Group B** As above **T**	**Group C** As above **T**	**Group D** As above **I**	**Group E** As above **I**	**Group A** As above **OA**	**Group D** Read sentences.

Fitting in with the National Literacy Framework

Word work: W8 to secure understanding and use of the terms *vowel* and *consonant*; **W6** to read on sight high frequency words likely to occur in graded texts.

Sentence work: S6 to use simple organizational devices to indicate sequences and relationships; **S4** to reread own writing for sense and punctuation.

Text work: T18 to use appropriate register in writing instructions; **T12** to use simple poetry structures and to substitute own ideas.

T = Teacher   **I = Independent**   **OA = Other adult**

These weekly plans are intended as exemplars only and teachers will want to exercise their own skill and judgement when planning for the Literacy Hour.

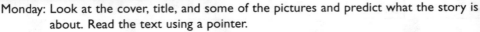
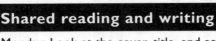

Stage 7   Red Planet   Year 2 Term 2

Shared reading and writing

Monday: Look at the cover, title, and some of the pictures and predict what the story is about. Read the text using a pointer.

Tuesday: Read the story using discussion pointers from *Teacher's Guide 3* on pages 57–58.

Wednesday: Recall how they escaped from the cave. Find and reread that part of the story together. Use some general discussion ideas from page 59 *Teacher's Guide 3*.

Thursday: Cover *they*, *he*, *we* and *I* on pages 12–14. Read the text and decide which pronoun is missing. How can you tell? Explain how you know which to use.

Friday: Shared writing: Explain what themes are. Talk about themes in familiar stories. Discuss and plan another story with a space theme. How will it begin? Who will it be about? Where will they be? What will happen?

Word work

The common spelling patterns for the phonemes *air*, *or*, and *er*. Practise matching the verb to the pronoun.

Monday: Think of words that rhyme with *air*. List the words then sort them out according to spelling pattern: *bear*, *care*, *fair*, *there*.

Tuesday: Think of words that rhyme with *paw*. Make a list then sort them out according to spelling pattern: *paw*, *more*, *door*, *caught*.

Wednesday: List words with *er* phoneme: *bigger*, *were*, *bird*, *fur*. Sort out the list according to spelling patterns.

Thursday: Change *We* to *I* or *She* in sentences such as 'We are going to land on that planet.' What other changes are needed?

Friday: Practise spelling or reading high frequency words or spelling patterns learned this week.

Guided group tasks (reading or writing)

Reading: Look at a variety of familiar books and decide what the theme is. Ask the children which themes they prefer. Read the story independently. Which words in the story match the space theme?

Writing: Find and list words from the story that match the space theme, e.g. *planet*, *spacesuit*, *rocket*.

Independent activities

1: Use Stage 7 workbooks or read familiar books.

Group Activity Sheets Book 3: Use the notes on page 45 to introduce the following:

2: Word work (page 46) common spelling patterns for the phonemes *air*, *or*, and *er*.

3: Sentence work (page 47) to be aware of the need for grammatical agreement in speech and writing.

4: Text work (page 48) to discuss and compare story themes.

5: The creature game on page 79 of *Teacher's Guide 3*; or read playscript.

Plenary

Use this time to allow children to explain their work to others. It is also an opportunity to reinforce teaching points as they arise and to add to the morning's word work.

Suggested Weekly Plan — RED PLANET — STAGE 7 — YEAR 2 TERM 2

	Whole class – shared reading and writing.	Whole class – phonics, spelling, vocabulary, grammar.	Guided group tasks (reading or writing)	Guided group tasks (reading or writing)	Independent group tasks	Independent group tasks	Independent group tasks	Plenary
Mon	Predict story from cover and pictures. Read the story.	Think of words that rhyme with *air*. Sort according to spelling pattern: *bear, care, fair, there*.	**Group A** Guided reading. Themes, GAS Bk3 p48.	**Group B** Workbook or read familiar book. Guided reading.	**Group C** Agreement in sentences, GAS Bk3 p47.	**Group D** The creature game, TG3 p79.	**Group E** Phonemes *air, er, or*, GAS Bk3 p46.	**Group E** Talk about phonemes work. Add more words to word work lists.
			T	T	I	I	OA	
Tues	Read the story using discussion pointers, TG3 p57–58.	*or* phonemes: *or, paw, more, door, caught*. Find more for each pattern by changing onsets.	**Group E** As above	**Group A** As above	**Group B** As above	**Group C** As above	**Group D** As above	**Group D** Talk about phonemes work. Add more words to word work lists.
			T	T	I	I	OA	
Wed	Recall how they escaped from the cave. Read that part together. Use general discussion, TG3 p59.	*er* phonemes: *bigger, computer*. Also: *were, bird, fur*. Make lists with same spelling patterns.	**Group D** As above	**Group E** As above	**Group A** As above	**Group B** Word lotto Stage 4 or 5, Games Box 4–5.	**Group C** As above	**Group A** Read sentences and check for agreement.
			T	T	I	I	OA	
Thur	Cover *They, he, we* and *I* on pages 12–14. Read the text and decide which pronoun is missing each time.	Change pronoun in sentences such as 'We are going to land on that planet.' Change verb to agree.	**Group C** As above	**Group D** As above	**Group E** As above	**Group A** As above	**Group B** As above	**Group C** Explain work with themes.
			T	T	I	I	OA	
Fri	Talk about themes in stories. Discuss and plan another story with a space theme.	Practise/revise this week's high frequency words.	**Group B** As above	**Group C** As above	**Group D** As above	**Group E** As above	**Group A** As above	**Group B** Explain work about themes. Read ideas for a space story.
			T	T	I	I	OA	

Fitting in with the National Literacy Framework

Word work: W2 the common spelling patterns for the vowel phonemes *air, or, er*.

Sentence work: S4 to be aware of the need for grammatical agreement in speech and writing, matching verbs to nouns/pronouns correctly.

Text work: T3 to discuss and compare story themes. **T13** to use story settings from reading, write a different story in the same setting.

T = Teacher   **I = Independent**   **OA = Other adult**

These weekly plans are intended as exemplars only and teachers will want to exercise their own skill and judgement when planning for the Literacy Hour.

Lost in the Jungle
Roderick Hunt   Alex Brychta

Stage 7   Lost in the Jungle   Year 2 Term 2

Shared reading and writing

Monday: Look at the cover, title, and some of the pictures and predict what the story is about. Read the text using a pointer. Read with pace and expression.

Tuesday: Read the story using discussion pointers from *Teacher's Guide 3* on pages 60–62.

Wednesday: Explain 'settings' to the children. Find out where the setting changes from home to the jungle and from the jungle to the Lost City. Read the story for one setting. Use some of the general discussion points on page 62 *Teacher's Guide 3*.

Thursday: Retell the main points of the story that tell how they found the Lost City. Read the part from the rope bridge to the end.

Friday: Shared writing: Choose one of the three settings for this story. Write a plan for a new story in this setting.

Word work

To split familiar compound words into their component parts.

Monday: Use the words listed on page 50 *Group Activity Sheets Book 3* as examples. Show the children that each word can be split into two whole words. Write the two separate words.

Tuesday: Think of more compound words. Use a dictionary to help, e.g. by looking up *water* and finding *waterlogged*, *waterproof*, and *watertight*.

Wednesday: Find more compound words beginning with *any*, *every*, *some*.

Thursday: Practise spelling compound words by breaking them into parts, then using phonemes.

Friday: Practise spelling or reading high frequency words or spelling patterns learned this week.

Guided group tasks (reading or writing)

Reading: Introduce the book then remind the children about settings. Ask them to find different settings within the story. Read independently.

Writing: Start an individual collection of compound words, splitting them into their component parts for spelling.

Independent activities

1: Use Stage 7 workbooks or read familiar books.

Group Activity Sheets Book 3: Use the notes on page 49 to introduce the following:

2: Word work (page 50) split familiar compound words into their component parts.

3: Sentence work (page 51) to use verb tenses with increasing accuracy; to use the past tense for narration.

4: Text work (page 52) to discuss story settings.

5: Word hunt game from *Teacher's Guide 3* Owls Activity Sheet 34; or read playscript.

Plenary

Use this time to allow children to explain their work to others. It is also an opportunity to reinforce teaching points as they arise and to add to the morning's word work.

Suggested Weekly Plan   LOST IN THE JUNGLE   STAGE 7   YEAR 2 TERM 2

	Whole class – shared reading and writing.	Whole class – phonics, spelling, vocabulary, grammar.	Guided group tasks (reading or writing)	Guided group tasks (reading or writing)	Independent group tasks			Plenary
Mon	Predict story from title and pictures. Read the story.	Use compound words from GAS Bk3 p50 to show how each word can be divided.	Group A — Guided reading. Compound words, GAS Bk3 p50. (T)	Group B — Workbook or read familiar book. Guided reading. (T)	Group C — Game from Games Box 6–9 or read playscript. (I)	Group D — Tenses in sentences, GAS Bk3 p51. (I)	Group E — Settings, GAS Bk3 p52. (OA)	Group A — Read and list compound words.
Tues	Read the story. Use discussion pointers, TG3 p60–62.	Find compound words in text. Use dictionary to find more 'water' words.	Group E — As above (T)	Group A — As above (T)	Group B — As above (I)	Group C — As above (I)	Group D — As above (OA)	Group C — Explain change of tense in sentences.
Wed	Explain 'settings'. Find three different settings in the story. Read part of the story.	Use dictionary to find compound words beginning with *any, every, some.*	Group D — As above (T)	Group E — As above (T)	Group A — As above (I)	Group B — Word lotto Stage 4 or 5, Games Box 4–5. (I)	Group C — As above (OA)	Group D — Read compound words list. Find more beginning with *snow.*
Thur	Retell the main points in finding the Lost City from the rope bridge onwards.	Practise breaking compound words into parts. Use phonemes to support spelling.	Group C — As above (T)	Group D — As above (T)	Group E — As above (I)	Group A — As above (I)	Group B — As above (OA)	Group B — Explain work on settings.
Fri	Choose a setting from this story. Write a plan for a new story in this setting.	Practise/revise this week's high frequency words.	Group B — As above (T)	Group C — As above (T)	Group D — As above (I)	Group E — As above (I)	Group A — As above (OA)	Group E — Read sentences with changed tenses.

Fitting in with the National Literacy Framework

Word work: W4 to split familiar compound words into their component parts; **W2** to segment words into phonemes for spelling.

Sentence work: S5 to use verb tenses with increasing accuracy in speaking and writing and to use the past tense consistently for narration.

Text work: T5 to discuss story settings; to compare differences; to locate key words and phrases in text; **T13** to use story settings from reading to write a different story in the same setting.

T = Teacher   I = Independent   OA = Other adult

These weekly plans are intended as exemplars only and teachers will want to exercise their own skill and judgement when planning for the Literacy Hour.

Stage 7   The Broken Roof   Year 2 Term 2

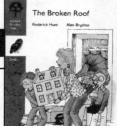

Shared reading and writing

Monday: Look at the cover, title, and some of the pictures, and predict what the story is about. Read the text.

Tuesday: Read the story using discussion pointers from *Teacher's Guide 3* on pages 63–64.

Wednesday: Retell the story. Use the general discussion ideas on page 65 of *Teacher's Guide 3*. Encourage the children to express their own thoughts and opinions.

Thursday: Shared writing: Look at the pictures on pages 16 and 17. Cover the text with plain paper. What did the children say to each other? Ask the children to suggest what was said while the teacher scribes. Vary the words used for *said*.

Friday: Compare Biff, Chip and Kipper with Victoria, Edward, and Will. How are they alike? How are they different?

Word work

Discriminate syllables in words.

Monday: Explain syllables by clapping the patterns of children's names. Count the syllables each time. Sort and list names with one, two, three, or four syllables.

Tuesday: Find words in the text with one, two, or three syllables. Say and clap the patterns to check.

Wednesday: Break words from the text and from the high frequency list into syllables. Use phonemes to spell the words.

Thursday: Find the longest words in the text and break them into syllables. Use phonemes to spell them.

Friday: Practise spelling or reading high frequency words or spelling patterns learned this week.

Guided group tasks (reading or writing)

Reading: Introduce the book, using the title and cover to predict what the story is about. Read the story independently. Find pages with speech marks. Discuss what these mean and how they affect reading aloud.

Writing: Practise using speech marks to show what is being said. Either make up sentences or use some from the story. Teach the children how to put in speech marks correctly.

Independent activities

1: Use Stage 7 workbooks or read familiar books.

Group Activity Sheets Book 3: Use the notes on page 53 to introduce the following:

2: Word work (page 54) to discriminate syllables in multi-syllabic words.

3: Sentence work (page 55) to identify speech marks in reading, understand their purpose and use the term correctly.

4: Text work (page 56) to identify and describe characters.

5: Word jigsaw from *Teacher's Guide 3* Activity Sheet 1; or read playscript.

Plenary

Use this time to allow children to explain their work to others. It is also an opportunity to reinforce teaching points as they arise and to add to the morning's word work.

Suggested Weekly Plan   THE BROKEN ROOF   STAGE 7   YEAR 2 TERM 2

Day	Whole class – shared reading and writing	Whole class – phonics, spelling, vocabulary, grammar	Guided group tasks (reading or writing)	Guided group tasks (reading or writing)	Independent group tasks	Independent group tasks	Independent group tasks	Plenary
Mon	Predict story from title and cover. Read the story.	Introduce syllables. Clap the syllables and count syllables in children's names.	**Group A** Guided reading. Syllables, GAS Bk3 p54. (T)	**Group B** Workbook or read familiar book. Guided reading. (T)	**Group C** Characters, GAS Bk3 p56.	**Group D** Playscript or word jigsaw, TG3 AS 12.	**Group E** Speech marks, GAS Bk3 p55.	**Group A** Talk about syllables in names for their group and show work.
Tues	Read the story. Use discussion pointers, TG3 p63–64.	Find words in the text with one, two, or three syllables. Make lists of words found.	**Group E** As above (T)	**Group A** As above (T)	**Group B** As above	**Group C** As above (I)	**Group D** As above (OA)	**Group E** Talk about syllables in names for their group and show work.
Wed	Retell the story. Use general discussion ideas from TG3 p65.	Break words from the text into syllables, use phonemes to spell them.	**Group D** As above (T)	**Group E** As above (T)	**Group A** As above	**Group B** Word lotto Stage 4 or 5, Games Box 4–5. (I)	**Group C** As above (OA)	**Group C** Explain speech marks work.
Thur	Shared writing. Cover text on pages 16 and 17. Write what the children are saying.	Find longer words from text. Use syllables and phonemes to spell them.	**Group C** As above (T)	**Group D** As above (T)	**Group E** As above (I or OA)	**Group A** As above (I)	**Group B** As above (OA)	**Group B** Explain speech marks work.
Fri	Compare Biff, Chip, Kipper with Victoria, Edward, Will. Similarities, differences.	Practise/revise this week's high frequency words or spelling patterns.	**Group B** As above (T)	**Group C** As above (T)	**Group D** As above (I or OA)	**Group E** As above (I)	**Group A** As above (OA or I)	**Group D** Talk about characters in the story.

Fitting in with the National Literacy Framework

Word work: W5 to discriminate orally, syllabic words using children's names and words from their reading; **W2** to segment words into phonemes for spelling.

Sentence work: S6 to identify speech marks in reading, understand their purpose, use the term correctly.

Text work: T6 to identify and describe characters, expressing own views; **T14** to write character profiles using key words and phrases that describe or are spoken by characters in the text.

T = Teacher   **I = Independent**   **OA = Other adult**

These weekly plans are intended as exemplars only and teachers will want to exercise their own skill and judgement when planning for the Literacy Hour.

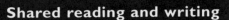

Stage 7   The Lost Key   Year 2 Term 2

Shared reading and writing

Monday: Look at the cover, title, and some of the pictures, and predict what the story is about. Read the text. For new words remind the children how to read ahead then reread the sentence to make sense of the text.

Tuesday: Read the story using discussion pointers from *Teacher's Guide 3* on pages 66–68.

Wednesday: Retell the story. Use the general discussion ideas on page 68 of *Teacher's Guide 3*. Encourage the children to express their ideas and own opinions.

Thursday: Shared writing: Make speech bubbles for characters illustrated on pages 14–17. Cover the text and decide what they are saying. The teacher scribes. Compare speech bubbles with the text.

Friday: Ask children to read one scene from *The Lost Key* playscript. Find that part in the story and read the text. Compare the play with the story.

Word work

Words with *un* or *dis* prefixes.

Monday: Use the words listed on page 58 of *Group Activity Sheets Book 3* to discuss how words with these prefixes change their meanings.

Tuesday: Spell words listed yesterday with *un* and *dis* prefixes. Put the words into sentences.

Wednesday: Use a dictionary to look for more words with *un* and *dis* prefixes.

Thursday: Vocabulary extension: List all the words children can think of that could be used instead of *said*. Use a thesaurus to find some more.

Friday: Practise spelling or reading high frequency words or spelling patterns learned this week.

Guided group tasks (reading or writing)

Writing: Read the story independently. Discuss the difference between themes (what the overall story is about) and settings (where the story happens), decide what the theme and settings are for *The Lost Key*.

Writing: Use *The Lost Key* playscripts and choose one scene. Discuss how to change the dialogue in the play to conversation in a story. Revise use of speech marks and various words for *said*.

Independent activities

1: Use Stage 7 workbooks or read familiar books.

Group Activity Sheets Book 3: Use the notes on page 57 to introduce the following:

2: Word work (page 58) to spell words with the prefixes *un* and *dis* to indicate the negative.

3: Sentence work (page 59) to investigate other ways of presenting texts.

4: Text work (page 60) to use story settings from reading in own writing.

5: Retell the story using *The Lost Key* Activity Sheet 13 in *Teacher's Guide 3*. Children can be asked to order and match the text and the pictures or to use the pictures and write their own text.

Plenary

Use this time to allow children to explain their work to others. It is also an opportunity to reinforce teaching points as they arise and to add to the morning's word work.

Suggested Weekly Plan — THE LOST KEY — STAGE 7 — YEAR 2 TERM 2

Day	Whole class – shared reading and writing.	Whole class – phonics, spelling, vocabulary, grammar.	Guided group tasks (reading or writing)	Guided group tasks (reading or writing)	Independent group tasks	Independent group tasks	Independent group tasks	Plenary
Mon	Predict story from title and cover. Read the story.	Words with *un* or *dis* prefixes. Use words on GAS Bk3 p58 to show how meaning changes.	**Group A** Guided reading. Prefixes *un, dis*, GAS Bk3 p58.	**Group B** Workbook or read familiar book. Guided reading or writing.	**Group C** Writing speech bubbles. Use text to help.	**Group D** Playscript or *The Lost Key* TG3 AS13. Order or retell story.	**Group E** (least able) Story writing, GAS Bk3 p60.	**Group A** Read *un* and *dis* prefix work.
Tues	Read the story using discussion pointers from TG3 p66–68.	Spell words with *un* and *dis* prefixes. Put them into sentences.	**Group E** As above	**Group A** As above	**Group B** As above	**Group C** As above	**Group D** As above — OA	**Group B** Talk about speech bubbles work.
Wed	Retell the story. Use general discussion ideas from TG3 p68.	Use dictionary to find more words with *un* and *dis* prefixes. List words.	**Group D** As above	**Group E** As above	**Group A** As above	**Group B** Word lotto Stage 4 or 5, Games Box 4–5.	**Group C** As above — OA	**Group D** Read prefix work. Read lists made earlier.
Thur	Write speech bubbles for pp14–17. Compare with the speech written in the story.	Vocabulary extension: list words for *said*. Replace *said* in text with variations.	**Group C** As above	**Group D** As above	**Group E** As above	**Group A** As above	**Group B** As above — OA	**Group B** Read stories.
Fri	Compare parts of playscript with story.	Practise/revise this week's high frequency words.	**Group B** As above	**Group C** As above	I or OA — **Group D** As above	**Group E** As above	OA or I — **Group A** As above	**Group A** Read stories.

T markers appear in guided group columns; I markers appear in independent group columns; OA and I or OA / OA or I as shown.

Fitting in with the National Literacy Framework

Word work: W8 to spell words with common prefixes, e.g. *un, dis* to indicate the negative.

Sentence work: S7 to investigate and recognize a range of ways of presenting texts, e.g. speech bubbles; **S6** to identify speech marks in reading, understand their purpose, use the term correctly.

Text work: T13 to use story settings from reading, e.g. write a different story in the same setting.

T = Teacher **I = Independent** **OA = Other adult**

These weekly plans are intended as exemplars only and teachers will want to exercise their own skill and judgement when planning for the Literacy Hour.

Stage 7   The Motorway   Year 2 Term 2

Shared reading and writing

Monday: Look at the cover, title, and some of the pictures and predict what the story is about. Read the text to page 16. Use a variety of cues to read new words.

Tuesday: Recall the beginning of the story. Read together from pages 17 to 23. Predict how the story will end.

Wednesday: Retell the story so far, then read to the end. Use the general discussion ideas on page 72, *Teacher's Guide 3* to encourage children to express their ideas and opinions.

Thursday: Shared writing: Use the story to write a character study of Gran. Find phrases in the text, e.g. 'She was good fun'.

Friday: What kind of story is *The Motorway*? Is it a magic adventure story or an 'everyday' story? List each kind of story, using titles children know well.

Word work

Collect and discuss antonyms.

Monday: Find *good*, *near*, and *first* on page 6. Ask the children to suggest words that mean the opposite of these. Scan the story for more words that have antonyms, e.g. on page 7, *higher*, *stronger*.

Tuesday: Collect more antonyms and use as a display or word bank.

Wednesday: Find and practise antonyms from Appendix List 1, e.g. *up*, *down*; *yes*, *no*; *new*, *old*.

Thursday: Vocabulary extension while practising commas in lists: e.g. Roads can be called lanes, avenues, streets, motorways. People can live in towns, cities ….

Friday: Practise spelling or reading high frequency words or spelling patterns learned this week.

Guided group tasks (reading or writing)

Reading: Read the story independently. Discuss meanings not directly stated in the text, e.g. How would the motorway spoil the village? How could flowers stop the motorway?

Writing: Plan a wall display of antonyms. Write the antonyms clearly for everyone to read. Use pens for colour, but remember size and accuracy.

Independent activities

1: Read familiar books.

Group Activity Sheets Book 3: Use the notes on page 61 to introduce the following:

2: Word work (page 62) to collect antonyms and discuss their meaning.

3: Sentence work (page 63) to use commas to separate items in a list.

4: Text work (page 64) to use dictionaries to locate words by using initial letter.

5: Assess Appendix List 1 words (*Group Activity Sheets Book 3* pages 124, 125) if another adult is available or choose game from Games Box Stages 6–9.

Plenary

Use this time to allow children to explain their work to others. It is also an opportunity to reinforce teaching points as they arise and to add to the morning's word work.

Suggested Weekly Plan — THE MOTORWAY — STAGE 7 — YEAR 2 TERM 2

	Whole class – shared reading and writing.	Whole class – phonics, spelling, vocabulary, grammar.	Guided group tasks (reading or writing)	Guided group tasks (reading or writing)	Independent group tasks			Plenary
Mon	Predict story from title and cover. Read text to page 16.	Antonyms, p6. Think of antonym for *good, near, first*. Continue on p7, *higher* etc.	**Group A** Guided reading. Antonyms, GAS Bk3 p62. (T)	**Group B** Read familiar book. Guided reading or writing. (T)	**Group C** Writing lists with commas, GAS Bk3 p63. (I)	**Group D** Dictionary work, GAS Bk3 p64. (I)	**Group E** Assess reading/ spelling of Appendix List 1 words. (OA)	**Group C** Show lists and explain use of commas.
Tues	Read story together to page 23. Predict how the story will end.	Collect more antonyms and use as a display or word bank.	**Group E** As above (T)	**Group A** As above (T)	**Group B** As above (I)	**Group C** As above (I)	**Group D** As above (OA)	**Group B** Explain work with lists and commas.
Wed	Finish reading the story together. Use general discussion, TG3 p72.	Practise spelling antonyms from Appendix List 1 words, e.g. *up/down, no/yes, new/old*.	**Group D** As above (T)	**Group E** As above (T)	**Group A** As above (I)	**Group B** As above (I)	**Group C** As above (OA)	**Group D** Explain antonyms work.
Thur	Write character study of Gran. Use words direct from text. Teacher scribes.	Vocabulary extension: commas in lists. Words for where people live, for roads, names of flowers.	**Group C** As above (T)	**Group D** As above (T)	**Group E** As above (I)	**Group A** As above (I)	**Group B** As above (OA)	**Group A** Explain dictionary work.
Fri	Is this a magic story or a story about everyday life? List magic and 'everyday' stories.	Practise/revise this week's high frequency words.	**Group B** As above (T)	**Group C** As above (T)	**Group D** As above (I)	**Group E** As above (I)	**Group A** As above (OA)	**Group E** Explain dictionary work.

Fitting in with the National Literacy Framework

Word work: W11 the use of antonyms: collect, discuss differences of meaning, and their spelling; **W2** to segment words into phonemes for spelling; **W10** new words linked to particular topics.

Sentence work: S8 to use commas to separate items in a list.

Text work: T16 to use dictionaries to find words using initial letter; **T3** to discuss themes; **T14** to write character profiles using key words and phrases that describe or are spoken by characters.

T = Teacher   **I = Independent**   **OA = Other adult**

These weekly plans are intended as exemplars only and teachers will want to exercise their own skill and judgement when planning for the Literacy Hour.

Stage 7   The Bully   Year 2 Term 2

Shared reading and writing

Monday: Look at the cover, title, and some of the pictures and predict what the story is about. Read the text to page 13.

Tuesday: Recall the beginning of the story. Read together from pages 14 to 25. Predict how the story will end.

Wednesday: Take turns to read the whole story with pace and expression. Use the general discussion ideas on page 72, *Teacher's Guide 3*.

Thursday: Shared writing: 'All about bullies'. Why was Rosie a bully? Write a description of what bullies do.

Friday: Read 'All about bullies' written yesterday. Add more ideas. Discuss what you can do if you are being bullied.

Word work

Modelling handwriting joins. You could use word work time as a handwriting lesson each day this week.

Monday: Diagonal lines join letters without ascenders, e.g. *ai*, *ar*, *un*.

Tuesday: Horizontal joins for letters without ascenders, e.g. *ou*, *vi*, *wi*.

Wednesday: Diagonal joins for letters with ascenders, e.g. *ab*, *ul*, *it*.

Thursday: Horizontal joins for letters with ascenders, e.g. *ol*, *wh*, *ot*.

Friday: Practise spelling or reading high frequency words or spelling patterns learned this week.

Guided group tasks (reading or writing)

Reading: Assess sight recognition of words at Stage 7 using page 71, *Group Activity Sheets Book 3*.

Writing: Use a recent piece of writing and review content, spelling, or punctuation according to need.

Independent activities

1: Read familiar books.

Group Activity Sheets Book 3: Use the notes on page 65 to introduce the following:

2: Word work (page 70) to read and spell words with the digraphs *wh*, *ph*, *ch* (as in *Christopher*).

3: Word work (page 66) to use and practise the four basic handwriting joins.

4: Sentence work (page 67) to secure the use of simple sentences in own writing.

5: Text work (page 68): to write character profiles, e.g. posters.

Plenary

Use this time to allow children to explain their work to others. It is also an opportunity to reinforce teaching points as they arise and to add to the morning's word work.

Suggested Weekly Plan | THE BULLY | STAGE 7 | YEAR 2 TERM 2

	Whole class – shared reading and writing.	Whole class – phonics, spelling, vocabulary, grammar.	Guided group tasks (reading or writing)	Guided group tasks (reading or writing)	Independent group tasks			Plenary
Mon	Predict story from title and cover. Read text to p13.	Model handwriting joins using words from Appendix List 1. Practise spelling them.	**Group A** Guided reading. Wh, ph, ch wordsearch, GAS Bk3 p70. **T**	**Group B** Read familiar book. Assess words at Stage 7, GAS p71. **T**	**Group C** Sentences, GAS Bk3 p67. **I**	**Group D** Rosie poster, GAS Bk3 p68.	**Group E** Handwriting, GAS Bk3 p66.	**Group D** Read and show Rosie poster.
Tues	Recall story so far. What will happen next? Read together to p25. How will the story end?	As above with different joins.	**Group E** As above **T**	**Group A** As above **T**	**Group B** As above **I**	**Group C** As above	**Group D** As above **OA**	**Group B** Read sentences.
Wed	Take turns to read the story with expression and pace. Use general discussion questions, TG3 p72.	As above with different joins.	**Group D** As above **T**	**Group E** As above **T**	**Group A** As above **I**	**Group B** As above	**Group C** As above **OA**	**Group C** Show best handwriting.
Thur	All about bullies. Why was Rosie a bully? Write a description.	As above with different joins.	**Group C** As above **T**	**Group D** As above **T**	**Group E** As above **I**	**Group A** As above	**Group B** As above **OA**	**Group E** Read sentences.
Fri	Read yesterday's character description. Add more ideas.	Practise/revise this week's high frequency words.	**Group B** As above **T**	**Group C** As above **T**	**Group D** As above **I**	**Group E** As above	**Group A** As above **OA**	**Group A** Show best handwriting.

Fitting in with the National Literacy Framework

Word work: W14 to use and practise the four basic handwriting joins; **W3** to read and spell words with the digraphs wh, ph, ch (as in Christopher); **W7** to read on sight words likely to occur in graded texts.

Sentence work: S9 to secure the use of simple sentences in own writing.

Text work: T14 to write character profiles, e.g. simple posters using key words or phrases that describe or are spoken by characters in the text.

T = Teacher   **I = Independent**   **OA = Other adult**

These weekly plans are intended as exemplars only and teachers will want to exercise their own skill and judgement when planning for the Literacy Hour.

Stage 8   The Kidnappers   Year 2 Term 3

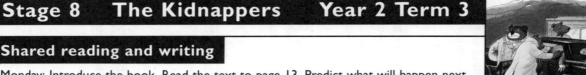

Shared reading and writing

Monday: Introduce the book. Read the text to page 13. Predict what will happen next. Read to the end. Was it as you predicted?

Tuesday: Take turns to read the whole story with pace and expression. Use the discussion pointers from page 137 *Teacher's Guide 3*.

Wednesday: Retell the story from memory. Use the general discussion ideas on page 138, *Teacher's Guide 3* to answer questions not directly answered in the text.

Thursday: Shared writing: Read the story again to page 7. Discuss the difference between fact and fiction. Ask the children for suggestions of each. Write two lists: facts in one, fiction in the other.

Friday: Read fact and fiction lists; add some more sentences to each list.

Word work

Synonyms and other words or phrases with similar meanings.

Monday: Find synonyms for words in the story, e.g. *sad*, *began* (p1) *ran*, *little* (p2) *beautiful* (p9). Read the sentences with the synonyms. Do they mean the same?

Tuesday: List more synonyms for words in the text. Each time replace the word with the synonym and read the sentence. Does the meaning stay the same?

Wednesday: Use a dictionary or a thesaurus to find more synonyms. Put each word in a sentence.

Thursday: Discuss shades of meaning in synonyms. Try two or three words in the same sentence and decide *which one is best, e.g. pretty, beautiful, lovely*.

Friday: Practise spelling or reading high frequency words or spelling patterns learned this week.

Guided group tasks (reading or writing)

Reading: Introduce the book. Read the story independently. Read page 30 together. Which words could be changed without changing the meaning?

Writing: Choose one page from the book (e.g. page 27). Rewrite it changing at least three words, but without changing the meaning. Work as a group.

Independent activities

1: Read familiar books or Magpies Stage 8 workbooks.

Group Activity Sheets Book 3: Use the notes on page 75 to introduce the following:

2: Word work (page 76) to use synonyms to express similar meaning.

3: Sentence work (page 77) to turn statements into questions using *wh* question words and question marks.

4: Text work (page 78) to understand the difference between fact and fiction; to use the terms *fact* and *fiction* appropriately.

5: Retell the story using Activity Sheet 3 'Mini-adventures (*The Kidnappers*)'. Cut up the page for the children to re-order and number. Make into little books by stapling the pages together or by mounting them on coloured paper.

Plenary

Use this time to allow children to explain their work to others. It is also an opportunity to reinforce teaching points as they arise and to add to the morning's word work.

Suggested Weekly Plan — THE KIDNAPPERS — STAGE 8 — YEAR 2 TERM 3

	Whole class – shared reading and writing.	Whole class – phonics, spelling, vocabulary, grammar.	Guided group tasks (reading or writing)	Guided group tasks (reading or writing)	Independent group tasks			Plenary
Mon	Predict story from title and cover. Read text to page 16. Make predictions. Read to end.	Synonyms. Think of words that mean the same as *sad, began, little, beautiful, lots* etc.	**Group A** (most able) Guided reading. Synonyms, GAS Bk3 p76. **T**	**Group B** Workbook or read familiar book. Guided reading. **T**	**Group C** Mini-adventures, *The Kidnappers*, TG3 Magpies AS3. **I**	**Group D** Fact or fiction? GAS Bk3 p78.	**Group E** (least able) Statements and questions, GAS Bk3 p77. **OA**	**Group A** Explain synonyms work.
Tues	Read the story using discussion pointers, TG3 p137.	List more synonyms for words in text or words suggested by children.	**Group E** As above **T**	**Group A** As above **T**	**Group B** As above **I**	**Group C** As above	**Group D** As above **OA**	**Group C** Read questions from statements. Read mini-adventures.
Wed	Retell the story. Use general discussion pointers from TG3 p138.	Use dictionaries to find more synonyms. Spell using syllables and phonemes.	**Group D** As above **T**	**Group E** As above **T**	**Group A** As above **I**	**Group B** As above	**Group C** As above **OA**	**Group D** Read synonyms work.
Thur	Shared writing. What are 'facts'? What is fiction? Write lists of examples of each.	Discuss shades of meaning in synonyms. Use in sentences and decide which sounds best.	**Group C** As above **T**	**Group D** As above **T**	**Group E** As above **I**	**Group A** As above	**Group B** As above **OA**	**Group B** Read and explain statements and questions work.
Fri	Add to lists of facts and fiction sentences. Refer to books read recently.	Practise/revise this week's high frequency words or spelling patterns.	**Group B** As above **T**	**Group C** As above **T**	**Group D** As above **I**	**Group E** As above	**Group A** As above **OA**	**Group E** Explain fact and fiction work.

Fitting in with the National Literacy Framework

Word work: W10 to use synonyms and other alternative words/phrases that express same or similar meanings.

Sentence work: S6 to turn statements into questions using *wh* questions and question marks; **S1** to read text aloud with intonation and expression appropriate to grammar and punctuation.

Text work: T13 to understand the distinction between fact and fiction; to use the terms *fact* and *fiction* appropriately.

T = Teacher   **I = Independent**   **OA = Other adult**

These weekly plans are intended as exemplars only and teachers will want to exercise their own skill and judgement when planning for the Literacy Hour.

Stage 8 Viking Adventure Year 2 Term 3

Shared reading and writing

Monday: Introduce the book. Read the text to page 17. Predict what will happen next. Read to the end. Was it as you predicted?

Tuesday: Reread the whole story with pace and expression. Use the discussion pointers from page 139 *Teacher's Guide 3*. Find the place in the text that answers some of the questions.

Wednesday: Retell the story from memory. Use the general discussion ideas on page 140 *Teacher's Guide 3* to answer questions not directly answered in the text.

Thursday: Shared writing: retell what happened to the children after the longship landed. Use the past tense consistently.

Friday: Discuss favourite magic key stories. Ask the children to give reasons for their choice. Is there a class favourite? Why do the children like this story best?

Word work

Revise syllables; consolidate work on standard forms of verbs.

Monday: Remind the children about syllables in words. Clap the title 'Viking Adventure' together. Choose words from the text and clap syllables.

Tuesday: Find the longest words in the story. Break down the words into syllables. Use phonemes to spell these words.

Wednesday: Cover all the verbs on pages 22–25. Read the text and ask the children to supply the correct form of the missing verbs. Spell them if possible.

Thursday: Practise using the correct form of the verb 'to be' by putting *be, is, are, was, were, being* into separate sentences.

Friday: Practise spelling or reading high frequency words or spelling patterns learned this week.

Guided group tasks (reading or writing)

Reading: Introduce the book. Read the story independently. What have you found out about the Vikings by reading this story? How could you check these ideas?

Writing: Make up a language puzzle for the rest of the class, e.g. How many words can be made using the vowels and consonants in 'adventure'? Work together to find out the maximum number of words so that you can give the other children a target.

Independent activities

1: Read familiar books or use Magpies Stage 8 workbooks.

Group Activity Sheets Book 3: Use the notes on page 79 to introduce the following:

2: Word work (page 80) to reinforce work on discriminating syllables.

3: Sentence work (page 81) to use the standard forms of verbs in writing and the past tense consistently for narration.

4: Text work (page 82) to invent language puzzles derived from reading.

5: Handwriting practise: Ask the children to copy part of the text or a poem in their best handwriting.

Plenary

Use this time to allow children to explain their work to others. It is also an opportunity to reinforce teaching points as they arise and to add to the morning's word work.

Suggested Weekly Plan VIKING ADVENTURE STAGE 8 YEAR 2 TERM 3

	Whole class – shared reading and writing.	Whole class – phonics, spelling, vocabulary, grammar.	Guided group tasks (reading or writing)	Guided group tasks (reading or writing)	Independent group tasks			Plenary
Mon	Predict story from title and cover. Read text to page 17. Predict rest of story. Read to end.	Revise syllables. Clap and count syllables in words from text.	**Group A** Guided reading. Syllables, GAS Bk3 p80. (T)	**Group B** Workbook or read familiar book. Guided reading. (T)	**Group C** Retell the story, GAS Bk3 p81. (I)	**Group D** Handwriting practice. (I)	**Group E** Language puzzle, GAS Bk 3 p82. (OA)	**Group E** Show and explain puzzles.
Tues	Reread the story. Use discussion pointers, TG3 p139. Find answers to some of the questions in text.	Choose words with three or four syllables. Work out phonemes for each syllable. Spell the word.	**Group E** As above (T)	**Group A** As above (T)	**Group B** As above (I)	**Group C** As above (I)	**Group D** As above (OA)	**Group B** Read retold stories. **Group C** Show handwriting.
Wed	Retell the story from memory. Use general discussion ideas from TG3 p140.	Cover verbs on pages 22–25. Ask children to suggest correct form of verb and spell it.	**Group D** As above (T)	**Group E** As above (T)	**Group A** As above (I)	**Group B** As above (I)	**Group C** As above (OA)	**Group D** Explain syllables work.
Thur	Retell what happened to the children after the longship landed. Use past tense.	Put correct form of verbs. Put *is*, *are*, *was*, *were*, *being* into sentences.	**Group C** As above (T)	**Group D** As above (T)	**Group E** As above (I)	**Group A** As above (I)	**Group B** As above (OA)	**Group A** Show handwriting work.
Fri	Discuss favourite magic key stories. Give reasons. Find class favourite.	Practise/revise this week's high frequency words or spelling patterns.	**Group B** As above (T)	**Group C** As above (T)	**Group D** As above (I)	**Group E** As above (I)	**Group A** As above (OA)	Read stories. Praise use of speech marks and spelling.

Fitting in with the National Literacy Framework

Word work: W2 to reinforce work on discriminating syllables in reading and spelling from previous terms.

Sentence work: S3 to use standard forms of verbs in writing and to use the past tense consistently for narration.

Text work: T11 to invent language puzzles derived from reading; **T4** to compare books by same author, to evaluate and form preferences, giving reasons.

T = Teacher **I = Independent** **OA = Other adult**

These weekly plans are intended as exemplars only and teachers will want to exercise their own skill and judgement when planning for the Literacy Hour.

Stage 8   The Rainbow Machine   Year 2 Term 3

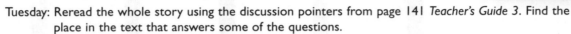

Shared reading and writing

Monday: Introduce the book. Read the text to page 16. Predict what will happen next. Read to the end. Was it as you predicted?

Tuesday: Reread the whole story using the discussion pointers from page 141 *Teacher's Guide 3*. Find the place in the text that answers some of the questions.

Wednesday: Retell the story together. Compare with the written text. Use the general discussion ideas on page 142 *Teacher's Guide 3* to answer questions not directly answered in the text.

Thursday: Discuss favourite parts of the story and read them again. Which parts are funny? Why do they make you laugh? Which ideas are especially unusual?

Friday: Shared writing: Write a book review of *The Rainbow Machine* together. Show children how to refer to the most humorous or original parts of the story.

Word work

Investigate words with the same spelling patterns but different sounds.

Monday: Use some of the words listed on page 84 of *Group Activity Sheets Book 3* to show that words may have the same spelling patterns but do not sound the same.

Tuesday: Add some more words to the lists started yesterday.

Wednesday: Practise spelling the words listed so far. Add more to the list.

Thursday: Change the onsets of common words and check whether or not they rhyme: e.g. *come, dome, home; here, there.*

Friday: Practise spelling or reading high frequency words or spelling patterns learned this week.

Guided group tasks (reading or writing)

Reading: Introduce the book. Read the story independently. Find all the different rainbows and ask children to think of a descriptive name for each one, e.g. 'The twisted candy rainbow.' Decide together which are the best suggestions and explain why.

Writing: Ask the children to explain how rainbows are made in this story. Write clearly using capital letters and full stops correctly.

Independent activities

1: Read familiar books or use Magpies Stage 8 workbooks.

Group Activity Sheets Book 3: Use the notes on page 83 to introduce the following:

2: Word work (page 84) to investigate words with the same spelling patterns but different sounds.

3: Sentence work (page 85) to write in clear sentences using capital letters and full stops correctly.

4: Text work (page 86) to read and respond imaginatively to humorous stories.

5: Mini-adventures: Magpies Activity Sheet 6: Ask the children to put the story in order and number the pages to make a little book. (They could staple the pages or mount them on coloured paper.) Alternative activity – read a playscript.

Plenary

Use this time to allow children to explain their work to others. It is also an opportunity to reinforce teaching points as they arise and to add to the morning's word work.

Suggested Weekly Plan — THE RAINBOW MACHINE — STAGE 8 — YEAR 2 TERM 3

	Whole class – shared reading and writing.	Whole class – phonics, spelling, vocabulary, grammar.	Guided group tasks (reading or writing)	Guided group tasks (reading or writing)	Independent group tasks	Independent group tasks	Independent group tasks	Plenary
Mon	Predict story from title and cover. Read text to page 16. Predict what happens next. Read to the end.	Words with same spelling patterns, different sounds. Use words from GAS Bk3 p84.	**Group A** Guided reading. Spelling patterns, GAS Bk3 p84. T	**Group B** Workbook or read familiar book. Guided reading. T	**Group C** All about Fred sentences, GAS Bk3 p85. I	**Group D** Playscript or put the story in order, mini-adventure TG3 Magpies AS6. I	**Group E** Weather machine story writing, GAS Bk3 p86.	**Group C** Read sentences about Fred.
Tues	Use discussion pointers, TG3 p141, while reading. Find answers to some questions in the text.	Extend lists of words that have common spelling patterns but different sounds.	**Group E** As above. T	**Group A** As above. T	**Group B** As above. I	**Group C** As above. I	**Group D** As above. OA	**Group E** Explain spelling patterns work.
Wed	Retell story together. Compare retelling with written text. Use general discussion, TG3 p142.	Practise spelling words with common spelling patterns.	**Group D** As above. T	**Group E** As above. T	**Group A** As above. I	**Group B** As above. I	**Group C** As above. OA	**Group D** Explain spelling patterns work.
Thur	Discuss favourite parts of the story. Which parts are funny? Why? Which ideas are especially good?	Change onset of various spelling patterns and see if the words sound the same, e.g. home, dome, come.	**Group C** As above. T	**Group D** As above. T	**Group E** As above. I	**Group A** As above. I	**Group B** As above. OA	**Group B** Read weather machine stories.
Fri	Write a book review together. Refer to original ideas and humour.	Practise/revise this week's high frequency words or spelling patterns.	**Group B** As above. T	**Group C** As above. T	**Group D** As above. I	**Group E** As above. I	**Group A** As above. OA	**Group A** Read weather machine stories.

Fitting in with the National Literacy Framework

Word work: W6 to investigate words that have the same spelling pattern but different sounds; **W1** to secure phonemic spelling from previous five terms.

Sentence work: S5 to write in clear sentences using capital letter and full stops accurately.

Text work: T6 to read and respond imaginatively to humorous stories; **T12** to write simple evaluations of books read and discussed giving reasons.

T = Teacher   **I = Independent**   **OA = Other adult**

These weekly plans are intended as exemplars only and teachers will want to exercise their own skill and judgement when planning for the Literacy Hour.

Stage 8   The Flying Carpet   Year 2 Term 3

Shared reading and writing

Monday: Introduce the book. Read the text to page 16. Predict what will happen next. Read to the end. Was it as you predicted?

Tuesday: Reread the whole story using the discussion pointers from page 143 *Teacher's Guide 3*. Use the text to check that the answers are right.

Wednesday: Retell the story together. Compare with the written text. Use the general discussion ideas on page 144 *Teacher's Guide 3* to answer questions not directly answered in the text.

Thursday: Shared writing: Discuss and write a review of *The Magic Carpet*. Why will other children enjoy this book?

Friday: Remind the children about settings for stories. Where does this story seem to be set? Which clues suggest another country?

Word work

Spelling words with the suffix *ly*.

Monday: Use the words listed on page 88 of *Group Activity Sheets Book 3* as examples. Add *ly* to the words listed. Discuss how it changes the meaning.

Tuesday: Read yesterday's lists and add some more words with *ly*. Put pairs of words (e.g. *bad, badly*) into separate sentences to show change of meaning .

Wednesday: Practise spelling words with *ly* endings. Use syllables and phonemes for more difficult words.

Thursday: Read page 18. Ask the children to find five words that can be changed by adding *ly*. Make up a sentence with each new word in it.

Friday: Practise spelling or reading high frequency words or spelling patterns learned this week.

Guided group tasks (reading or writing)

Reading: Introduce the book. Read the story independently. Find *prisoner* and *hostage* in the story. Discuss with the children how you can use the story to find out what these words mean.

Writing: Make up and write sentences using names from the group and using *his* or *her* correctly.

Independent activities

1: Read familiar books or use Magpies Stage 8 workbooks.

Group Activity Sheets Book 3: Use the notes on page 87 to introduce the following:

2: Word work (page 88) to spell words with the suffix *ly*.

3: Sentence work (page 89) as to the need for grammatical agreement, matching verbs to nouns and pronouns; using simple gender forms.

4: Text work (page 90) to use phonological, contextual, grammatical, and graphic knowledge to work out, predict, and check the meanings of unfamiliar words and to make sense of what they read.

5: Mini-adventures: Magpies Activity Sheet 5: put the story in order and number the pages. Staple the pages to make a book or mount on coloured paper if time. Alternative activity – read a playscript.

Plenary

Use this time to allow children to explain their work to others. It is also an opportunity to reinforce teaching points as they arise and to add to the morning's word work.

Suggested Weekly Plan   THE FLYING CARPET   STAGE 8   YEAR 2 TERM 3

	Whole class – shared reading and writing.	Whole class – phonics, spelling, vocabulary, grammar.	Guided group tasks (reading or writing)	Guided group tasks (reading or writing)	Independent group tasks			Plenary
Mon	Predict story from title and cover. Read to page 19. What will happen next? Read to end.	Words with *ly*. Use list on GAS Bk3 p88 as examples.	**Group A** Guided reading, GAS Bk3 p88. *(T)*	**Group B** Workbook or read familiar book. Guided reading. *(T)*	**Group C** Agreement, GAS Bk3 p89. *(I)*	**Group D** Playscript or put the story in order; mini-adventure TG3 Magpies AS6. *(I)*	**Group E** Meanings of words, GAS Bk3 p90. *(OA)*	**Group E** Read word meanings work.
Tues	Reread the story. Use discussion pointers, TG3 p143. Use text to check answers.	Add more *ly* words. Put some of them in sentences.	**Group E** As above *(T)*	**Group A** As above *(T)*	**Group B** As above *(I)*	**Group C** As above *(I)*	**Group D** As above *(OA)*	**Group B** Read story with agreement of pronouns and verbs.
Wed	Retell the story from memory. Use general discussion, TG3 p144.	Practise spelling words with *ly*. Use phonological knowledge to spell more difficult words.	**Group D** As above *(T)*	**Group E** As above *(T)*	**Group A** As above *(I)*	**Group B** As above *(I)*	**Group C** As above *(OA)*	**Group D** Read story with *ly* words.
Thur	Shared writing: Discuss and write review of *The Magic Carpet*.	Read page 18. Change *bad, cruel, greedy, poor,* and *happy* by adding *ly*.	**Group C** As above *(T)*	**Group D** As above *(T)*	**Group E** As above *(I)*	**Group A** As above *(I)*	**Group B** As above *(OA)*	**Group C** Read story with *ly* words.
Fri	Remind the children about settings. Where is this story set? How can you tell?	Practise/revise this week's high frequency words or spelling patterns.	**Group B** As above *(T)*	**Group C** As above *(T)*	**Group D** As above *(I)*	**Group E** As above *(I)*	**Group A** As above *(OA)*	**Group A** Read word meanings work.

Fitting in with the National Literacy Framework

Word work: W7 to spell words with the suffix *ly*; W1 to secure phonemic spellings from previous five terms.

Sentence work: S2 the need for grammatical agreement, matching verbs to nouns and pronouns; using simple gender forms correctly.

Text work: T2 to use context to work out, predict, and check the meanings of unfamiliar words and make sense of it; T12 to write simple evaluations of books read and discussed, giving reasons; T13 to understand the difference between *fact* and *fiction*; to use the terms *fact* and *fiction* appropriately.

T = Teacher   I = Independent   OA = Other adult

These weekly plans are intended as exemplars only and teachers will want to exercise their own skill and judgement when planning for the Literacy Hour.

Stage 8   A Day in London   Year 2 Term 3

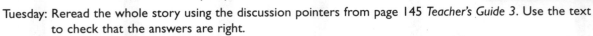

Shared reading and writing

Monday: Introduce the book. Read the text to page 17. Predict what will happen next. Read to the end. Was it as you predicted?

Tuesday: Reread the whole story using the discussion pointers from page 145 *Teacher's Guide 3*. Use the text to check that the answers are right.

Wednesday: Retell the story together. Compare with the written text. Use the general discussion ideas on page 146 *Teacher's Guide 3* to answer questions not directly answered in the text.

Thursday: Shared writing: Discuss children's days out in cities, towns, or theme parks. What are the best parts of these days out? Write a general account of 'Our best days out'.

Friday: Read yesterday's account of good days out. Add 'It is not so good when …' if children have stories of wet days, breakdowns, or accidents.

Word work

Discriminate, read, and spell the phonemes *ear* in *hear* and *ea* in *head*; discuss reasons for asking questions.

Monday: Make lists of words to rhyme with *head* and *hear* using the same spelling patterns.

Tuesday: Add more words to the lists. Practise spelling the words.

Wednesday: Put the words listed into sentences.

Thursday: Think of questions the children might ask during their day out, e.g. How long will it take to get there? Who was Nelson? How much is a ticket for the tube?

Friday: Practise spelling or reading high frequency words or spelling patterns learned this week.

Guided group tasks (reading or writing)

Reading: Introduce the book. Read the story independently. Talk about pages 30–32. What has happened that isn't in the story? Why do you think this was done?

Writing: Discuss pages 30–32 and write an explanation for the fact that the car is on a break-down truck.

Independent activities

1: Read familiar books or use Magpies Stage 8 workbooks.

Group Activity Sheets Book 3: Use the notes on page 91 to introduce the following:

2: Word work (page 92) to discriminate, read and spell the phonemes *ear* in *hear* and *ea* in *head*.

3: Sentence work (page 93) to compare a variety of questions from texts.

4: Text work (page 94) to plan and write sustained stories using their knowledge of story elements: narrative, settings, and the language of story.

5: Mini-adventures: Magpies Activity Sheet 7; put the story in order and number the pages.

Plenary

Use this time to allow children to explain their work to others. It is also an opportunity to reinforce teaching points as they arise and to add to the morning's word work.

Suggested Weekly Plan — A DAY IN LONDON — STAGE 8 — YEAR 2 TERM 3

	Whole class – shared reading and writing.	Whole class – phonics, spelling, vocabulary, grammar.	Guided group tasks (reading or writing)	Guided group tasks (reading or writing)	Independent group tasks			Plenary
Mon	Predict story from title and cover. Read to p17. What will happen next? Read to end.	The *ea* and *ear* phonemes. Make lists of words to rhyme with *head* and *ear*.	**Group A** Guided reading. An *ea* and *ear* wordsearch. **T**	**Group B** Workbook or read familiar book. Guided reading or writing. **T**	**Group C** Questions, GAS Bk3 p93. **I**	**Group D** Put the story in order, mini-adventure TG3 Magpies AS7. **I**	**Group E** Plan a story, GAS Bk3 p94. **I**	**Group A** Explain wordsearch.
Tues	Read the story using discussion pointers from TG3 p145.	Add more words to lists and practise spelling them.	**Group E** As above **T**	**Group A** As above **T**	**Group B** As above **I**	**Group C** As above **I**	**Group D** As above **OA**	**Group D** Read story plans.
Wed	Retell the story. Use general discussion ideas, TG3 p148.	Put *ea* and *ear* words into sentences.	**Group D** As above **T**	**Group E** As above **T**	**Group A** As above **I**	**Group B** As above **I**	**Group C** As above **OA**	**Group C** Read story plans.
Thur	Shared writing about children's days out in cities or towns. Teacher scribes.	Make up a variety of questions the children might have asked.	**Group C** As above **T**	**Group D** As above **T**	**Group E** As above **I**	**Group A** As above **I**	**Group B** As above **OA**	**Group E** Read questions.
Fri	Read above account. Add more, e.g. not so good days out.	Practise/revise this week's high frequency words or spelling patterns.	**Group B** As above **T**	**Group C** As above **T**	**Group D** As above **I**	**Group E** As above **I**	**Group A** As above **OA**	**Group B** Talk about wordsearch.

Fitting in with the National Literacy Framework

Word work: W3 to discriminate, read, and spell the phonemes *ear* (*hear*) and *ea* (*head*).

Sentence work: S7 to compare a variety of questions from texts; **S6** to turn statements into questions, learning a range of *wh* words typically used to open questions.

Text work: T10 to write sustained stories using their knowledge of story elements; **T13** to understand the difference between fact and fiction.

T = Teacher   **I = Independent**   **OA = Other adult**

These weekly plans are intended as exemplars only and teachers will want to exercise their own skill and judgement when planning for the Literacy Hour.

Stage 8   Victorian Adventure   Year 2 Term 3

Shared reading and writing

Monday: Introduce the book. Read the text to page 13. Predict what will happen next. Read to the end. Was it as you predicted?

Tuesday: Reread the whole story using the discussion pointers from page 147, *Teacher's Guide 3*. Use the text to check that the answers are right.

Wednesday: Retell the story together. Compare with the written text. Use the general discussion ideas on page 148 *Teacher's Guide 3* to answer questions not directly answered in the text.

Thursday: Shared writing: Find out about Queen Victoria from reference books. Show children how to use an index. Make a list of facts in whole sentences.

Friday: Read yesterday's work about Queen Victoria. Talk about fact and fiction. Can they make up some factual sentences based on the story, e.g. 'Blacksmiths make new shoes for horses.'

Word work

Revise the use of commas in lists; practise (or assess) reading and spelling all the high frequency words from Appendix List 1. You could make this a written assessment.

Monday: Remind children that items in a list within sentences have commas to separate them. You could list Kings and Queens the children know, or Magpies stories they have read, for example.

Tuesday: Revise or assess reading and spelling of high frequency words from Appendix List 1. These are listed in *Group Activity Sheets Book 3* pages 124 and 125.

Wednesday: Continue with revision or assessment.

Thursday: Continue with revision or assessment.

Friday: Continue with revision or assessment, or practise spelling or reading high frequency words or spelling patterns learned this week.

Guided group tasks (reading or writing)

Reading: Introduce the book. Read the story independently. Assess sight recognition of Stage 8 words. (Use the list on page 126 of *Group Activity Sheets Book 3*)

Writing: Review any recent piece of writing. Set targets and help that child to improve spelling, punctuation, content, or handwriting.

Independent activities

1: Read familiar books or use Magpies Stage 8 workbooks.

Group Activity Sheets Book 3: Use the notes on page 95 to introduce the following:

2: Word work (page 96) to secure spelling of all the high frequency words in Appendix List 1.

3: Sentence work (page 97) to use commas in lists.

4: Text work (page 98) to compare books by the same author: settings, characters, themes.

5: Mini-adventures: Magpies Activity Sheet 8: Put the story in order and number the pages.

Plenary

Use this time to allow children to explain their work to others. It is also an opportunity to reinforce teaching points as they arise and to add to the morning's word work.

Suggested Weekly Plan　　VICTORIAN ADVENTURE　STAGE 8　YEAR 2 TERM 3

	Whole class – shared reading and writing.	Whole class – phonics, spelling, vocabulary, grammar.	Guided group tasks (reading or writing)	Guided group tasks (reading or writing)	Independent group tasks			Plenary
Mon	Predict story from title and cover. Read to page 13. What will happen next? Read to end.	Remind children about use of commas in lists.	**Group A** Guided reading. Spell missing words, GAS Bk3 p96. _T_	**Group B** Workbook or read familiar book. Assessment, Stage 8 words. _T_	**Group C** Commas in lists, GAS Bk3 p97. _I_	**Group D** Put the story in order, mini-adventures, TG3 Magpies AS8. _I_	**Group E** Comparing stories, GAS Bk3 p98. _OA_	**Group A** Explain work and spell missing words.
Tues	Read the story using discussion pointers, TG3 p147. Find answers in the text.	Revise/assess spelling of high frequency words from Appendix List I, GAS Bk3 p124–5.	**Group E** As above _T_	**Group A** As above _T_	**Group B** As above _I_	**Group C** As above _I_	**Group D** As above _OA_	**Group E** Explain work and spell missing words.
Wed	Retell the story. Use general discussion, TG3 p148.	Continue spelling practice or assessment of above list.	**Group D** As above _T_	**Group E** As above _T_	**Group A** As above _I_	**Group B** As above _I_	**Group C** As above _OA_	**Group C** Read and explain comparisons of books by Roderick Hunt.
Thur	Find out and write facts about Queen Victoria. Model use of index in reference books.	Continue as above	**Group C** As above _T_	**Group D** As above _T_	**Group E** As above _I_	**Group A** As above _I_	**Group B** As above _OA_	**Group B** Read and explain comparisons of stories by Roderick Hunt.
Fri	Read work about Queen Victoria. Separate fact from fiction.	As above or revise this week's high frequency words or spelling patterns.	**Group B** As above _T_	**Group C** As above _T_	**Group D** As above _I_	**Group E** As above _I_	**Group A** As above _OA_	**Group D** Explain commas in lists.

Fitting in with the National Literacy Framework

Word work: W4 to secure spelling of high frequency words in Appendix List I; **W5** to read on sight high frequency words likely to occur in graded texts.

Sentence work: S4 to use commas in lists.

Text work: T4 to compare books by same author; **T15** to use contents page and index to get around text; **T13** to understand fact and fiction; to use terms _fact, fiction,_ and _non-fiction_ appropriately.

T = Teacher　　　**I** = Independent　　　**OA** = Other adult

These weekly plans are intended as exemplars only and teachers will want to exercise their own skill and judgement when planning for the Literacy Hour.

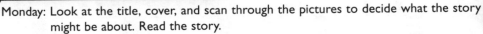
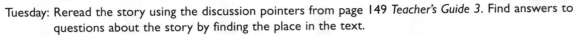

Stage 9   Green Island   Year 2 Term 3

Shared reading and writing

Monday: Look at the title, cover, and scan through the pictures to decide what the story might be about. Read the story.

Tuesday: Reread the story using the discussion pointers from page 149 *Teacher's Guide 3*. Find answers to questions about the story by finding the place in the text.

Wednesday: Use the questions listed for 'The story' in general discussion, page 150 *Teacher's Guide 3*, to recall events from the story and think of reasons.

Thursday: Read story. Use other discussion ideas to talk about islands, school visits, and conservation.

Friday: Shared writing: Note story elements from *Green Island*. Narrative: what are main points of story? Setting: where does it happen? Characters: who are the main characters? Dialogue: What does it tell us? Language of story: find phrases such as 'That night ...'., 'At the end of the week ...'.

Word work

Spell words with the suffix *ful*; composing questions.

Monday: Show the children how to change *care* into *careful*. Add *ful* to the words listed on page 100 *Group Activity Sheets Book 3*.

Tuesday: Add more *ful* words to the list. Put some of the words into sentences.

Wednesday: Practise reading and spelling *ful* words.

Thursday: Ask the children to make up some questions about the story using *who, what, when, where, why, how*. Find the answers in the text.

Friday: Practise spelling or reading high frequency words or spelling patterns learned this week.

Guided group tasks (reading or writing)

Reading: Introduce the book. Look at pages 20 and 21. What is toxic waste? Find another word for toxic in the picture. Read the story independently. Why was the toxic waste a problem?

Writing: Discuss the story the reporter wrote. What would be in the newspaper? What would the headlines be? Share ideas and begin to write the report.

Independent activities

1: Read familiar books or use Magpies Stage 9 workbooks.

Group Activity Sheets Book 3: Use the notes on page 99 to introduce the following:

2: Word work (page 100) to spell words with the suffix *ful*.

3: Sentence work (page 101) to turn statements into questions learning a range of *wh* question words to open questions.

4: Text work (page 102) to write their riddles and own language puzzles.

5: Rewrite the story independently from 'The children jumped out of the boat and went to look around the island.' What happened next? Retell in own words.

Plenary

Use this time to allow children to explain their work to others. It is also an opportunity to reinforce teaching points as they arise and to add to the morning's word work.

Suggested Weekly Plan — GREEN ISLAND — STAGE 9 — YEAR 2 TERM 3

	Whole class – shared reading and writing.	Whole class – phonics, spelling, vocabulary, grammar.	Guided group tasks (reading or writing)	Guided group tasks (reading or writing)	Independent group tasks			Plenary
Mon	Predict story from title and cover. Read the story.	Words with *ful* suffix. Use list on GAS Bk3 p100 as a starting point.	**Group A** Guided reading. Words ending with *ful*, GAS Bk3 p100.	**Group B** Workbook or read familiar book. Guided reading or writing.	**Group C** Word puzzles, GAS Bk3 p102.	**Group D** Rewrite the story of finding the toxic waste and the arrest.	**Group E** Questions from statements, GAS Bk3 p101.	**Group E** Read questions from statements.
Tues	Use discussion pointers, TG3 p149. Use text to check answers to questions.	Add words with *ful* suffix from other reading. Put them in sentences.	**Group E** As above	**Group A** As above	**Group B** As above	**Group C** As above	**Group D** As above	**Group B** Explain word puzzles.
Wed	Use general discussion ('The story'), TG3 p150, to recall incidents and reasons for them.	Practise reading and spelling words with *ful*.	**Group D** As above	**Group E** As above	**Group A** As above	**Group B** As above	**Group C** As above	**Group D** Read work with *ful* words. Spell some from memory.
Thur	Use remaining general discussion ideas, TG3 p150, to generate wider discussion.	Composing questions. Suggest questions about the story. List and spell question words.	**Group C** As above	**Group D** As above	**Group E** As above	**Group A** As above	**Group B** As above	**Group C** Read words with *ful*. Spell some from memory.
Fri	Use children's writing to develop use of story elements.	Practise/revise this week's high frequency words or spelling patterns.	**Group B** As above	**Group C** As above	**Group D** As above	**Group E** As above	**Group A** As above	**Group A** Read questions from statements.

T = Teacher   I = Independent   OA = Other adult

Fitting in with the National Literacy Framework

Word work: W7 to spell words with common suffixes, e.g. *ful*, *ly*.

Sentence work: S6 to turn statements into questions learning a range of *wh* words typically used to open questions.

Text work: T11 to write their own riddles and language puzzles; **T10** to write sustained stories, using their knowledge of story elements.

These weekly plans are intended as exemplars only and teachers will want to exercise their own skill and judgement when planning for the Literacy Hour.

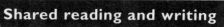

Stage 9   Storm Castle   Year 2 Term 3

Shared reading and writing

Monday: Look at the title, cover, and scan through the pictures to decide what the story might be about. Read the story to page 21. What will happen next?

Tuesday: Retell the beginning of the story. Read from page 22 to the end.

Wednesday: Reread the story using the discussion pointers from page 151 *Teacher's Guide 3*. Find answers to questions about the story in the text.

Thursday: Read the story from page 16 to the end. Use the general discussion ideas on page 152 *Teacher's Guide 3*, to generate talk about computers, robots, and mazes.

Friday: Shared writing: Read tongue twisters written by the children this week. Make up some more to fit this or other stories.

Word work

Use synonyms or other alternative words or phrases that express the same or similar meaning; to use standard form of verbs in writing.

Monday: Help children to explain what words mean, e.g. what is a robot? What does *favourite* mean? What is *danger*? Use dictionary to check meaning and compare definition with the children's explanations.

Tuesday: Look through the second half of the story and find more words to explain.

Wednesday: Verb forms: Cover the verbs on pages 16 and 17. Predict the missing verb and check that it sounds right in the sentence.

Thursday: Make up sentences using *was, were; came, come; bring, brought; buy, bought*. Check that the sentences make sense and sound right.

Friday: Practise spelling or reading high frequency words or spelling patterns learned this week.

Guided group tasks (reading or writing)

Reading: Introduce the book. Read the story independently. How did the children know the adventure would be in Storm Castle? Why didn't Biff like it much?

Writing: Think of words that describe how the children felt at different points in the story. Put them into sentences that would fit into the story, e.g. page 12, 'Chip was worried that the bridge might not be safe.'

Independent activities

1: Read familiar books or use Magpies Stage 9 workbooks.

Group Activity Sheets Book 3: Use the notes on page 103 to introduce the following:

2: Word work (page 104) to use synonyms and other alternative words or phrases that express the same or similar meanings.

3: Sentence work (page 105) to use standard forms of verbs in writing.

4: Text work (page 106) to write tongue twisters.

5: 'Look it up' Activity Sheet 13 *Teacher's Guide 3*: Finish sentences by referring to the text, or read playscript.

Plenary

Use this time to allow children to explain their work to others. It is also an opportunity to reinforce teaching points as they arise and to add to the morning's word work.

Suggested Weekly Plan — STORM CASTLE — STAGE 9 — YEAR 2 TERM 3

	Whole class – shared reading and writing.	Whole class – phonics, spelling, vocabulary, grammar.	Guided group tasks (reading or writing)	Guided group tasks (reading or writing)	Independent group tasks	Independent group tasks	Independent group tasks	Plenary
Mon	Predict story from title and cover. Read to p15. What will happen next?	Explain what words mean, e.g. *robot, favourite, exciting, danger, bridge* etc. Use dictionary to check and compare.	**Group A** Guided reading. Word meanings, GAS Bk3 p104. (T)	**Group B** Workbook or read familiar book. Guided reading or writing. (T)	**Group C** Correct verb form, GAS Bk3 p105. (I)	**Group D** Look it up, TG3. Magpies AS13. Complete the sentences. (I)	**Group E** Writing tongue twisters, GAS Bk3 p106. (OA)	**Group A** Read word meanings
Tues	Recall beginning of story. Read from p16 to end.	Choose words from second half of story. Explain meanings.	**Group E** As above (T)	**Group A** As above (T)	**Group B** As above (I)	**Group C** As above (I)	**Group D** As above (OA)	**Group D** Read tongue twisters.
Wed	Use discussion pointers, TG3 p151. Use text to check answers to questions.	Cover verbs on p16–17. Predict verb and check for correct form.	**Group D** As above (T)	**Group E** As above (T)	**Group A** As above (I)	**Group B** As above (I)	**Group C** As above (OA)	**Group C** Read tongue twisters.
Thur	Use general discussion ideas, TG3 p152, to generate wider discussion.	Make up sentences using *was, were; come, came; take, took; bring, brought, buy, bought.*	**Group C** As above (T)	**Group D** As above (T)	**Group E** As above (I)	**Group A** As above (I)	**Group B** As above (OA)	**Group E** Read sentences with correct verb form.
Fri	Read tongue twisters written this week. Write some more. Choose best words.	Practise/revise this week's high frequency words or spelling patterns.	**Group B** As above (T)	**Group C** As above (T)	**Group D** As above (I)	**Group E** As above (I)	**Group A** As above (OA)	**Group B** Read word meanings. Read class tongue twisters.

Fitting in with the National Literacy Framework

Word work: W10 to use synonyms and other alternative words and phrases that express the same or similar meanings.

Sentence work: S3 to use the standard forms of verbs in writing and to use the past tense consistently for narration.

Text work: T11 to write tongue twisters and alliterative sentences; **T9** to apply phonological, graphic knowledge, and sight recognition to spell words accurately.

T = Teacher   I = Independent   OA = Other adult

These weekly plans are intended as exemplars only and teachers will want to exercise their own skill and judgement when planning for the Literacy Hour.

Stage 9   Superdog   Year 2 Term 3

Shared reading and writing

Monday: Look at the title, cover, and scan through the pictures to decide what the story might be about. Read the story with pace and expression.

Tuesday: Reread the story using the discussion pointers from page 153 *Teacher's Guide 3*. Find answers to questions about the story in the text.

Wednesday: Read the story. Use the other discussion ideas from page 154 *Teacher's Guide 3* to generate talk about dog shows, superheroes, and playing with pets.

Thursday: Recall and retell one of Floppy's adventures. Compare oral and written versions.

Friday: Shared writing: Read book reviews written by the children this week. Remind the children how to check their own work. Is the spelling correct? Are there capital letters and full stops in the right places. Are there good ideas? Which ideas are the most interesting? Why?

Word work

Investigate words with the same spelling patterns but different sounds. Revise use of punctuation in sentences, including question marks and exclamation marks.

Monday: Think of and list words ending in *ear*. Separate the list into words that rhyme, e.g. *bear*, *pear*; *hear*, *fear*.

Tuesday: List words ending with *ush*. Sort into lists of words that rhyme with *rush* and those that rhyme with *push*.

Wednesday: Collect *ough* and *ought* words. Practise spelling these words.

Thursday: Make up sentences using full stops, exclamation marks, or question marks.

Friday: Practise spelling or reading high frequency words or spelling patterns learned this week.

Guided group tasks (reading or writing)

Reading: Introduce the book. Read the story independently. Why was Floppy called 'Superdog'? How was he the same as Superman? How was he different?

Writing: Make up another event where Floppy rescues someone. Write a few sentences to explain what happens. Write so that your event could fit into the book.

Independent activities

1: Read familiar books or use Magpies Stage 9 workbooks.

Group Activity Sheets Book 3: Use the notes on page 107 to introduce the following:

2: Word work (page 108) to investigate words with the same spelling patterns but different sounds.

3: Sentence work (page 109) to write in clear sentences using capital letters and full stops accurately.

4: Text work (page 110) to write simple evaluations of books read and discussed, giving reasons.

5: 'Look it up' Activity Sheet 14 *Teacher's Guide 3*: Finish writing sentences by referring to the script, or read a playscript.

Plenary

Use this time to allow children to explain their work to others. It is also an opportunity to reinforce teaching points as they arise and to add to the morning's word work.

Suggested Weekly Plan   SUPERDOG   STAGE 9   YEAR 2 TERM 3

	Whole class – shared reading and writing.	Whole class – phonics, spelling, vocabulary, grammar.	Guided group tasks (reading or writing)	Guided group tasks (reading or writing)	Independent group tasks			Plenary
Mon	Predict story from title and cover. Read the story with pace and expression.	Think of *ear* words. Sort into sets that rhyme, e.g. *bear, pear; hear, gear* etc.	**Group A** Guided reading. Spelling patterns, GAS Bk3 p108. T	**Group B** Workbook or read familiar book. Guided reading or writing. T	**Group C** Sentences, GAS Bk3 p109. I	**Group D** Look it up, TG3 Magpies AS14. Complete the sentences. I	**Group E** Review *Superdog*, GAS Bk3 p110. OA	**Group A** Explain spelling patterns work.
Tues	Use discussion pointers, TG3 p153. Use text to check answers to questions.	Think of *ush* words. Sort into sets that rhyme, e.g *rush, thrush; push, bush.* Repeat with *ull* words.	**Group E** As above T	**Group A** As above T	**Group B** As above I	**Group C** As above I	**Group D** As above OA	**Group D** Read book reviews.
Wed	Use general discussion ideas, TG3 p154, to generate wider discussion.	Collect *ough* and *ought* words. Make lists. Do any words rhyme? Practise spelling them.	**Group D** As above T	**Group E** As above T	**Group A** As above I	**Group B** As above I	**Group C** As above OA	**Group C** Read book reviews.
Thur	Recall and retell one of Floppy's adventures. Compare with the written text.	Revise punctuation in sentences. Make up sentences with full stops, question marks, and exclamation marks.	**Group C** As above T	**Group D** As above T	**Group E** As above I	**Group A** As above I	**Group B** As above OA	**Group E** Read sentences. Talk about punctuation.
Fri	Use reviews written this week to discuss /encourage personal responses.	Practise/revise this week's high frequency words or spelling patterns.	**Group B** As above T	**Group C** As above T	**Group D** As above I	**Group E** As above I	**Group A** As above OA	**Group B** Explain spelling pattern work.

Fitting in with the National Literacy Framework

Word work: W6 to investigate words with the same spelling patterns but different sounds.

Sentence work: S5 to write in clear sentences using capital letters and full stops correctly; **S1** to read text aloud with intonation and expression appropriate to the grammar and punctuation.

Text work: T12 to write simple evaluations of books read and discussed, giving reasons. **T3** to notice the difference between spoken and written forms through retelling known stories; compare oral versions with the written text.

T = Teacher   **I = Independent**   **OA = Other adult**

These weekly plans are intended as exemplars only and teachers will want to exercise their own skill and judgement when planning for the Literacy Hour.

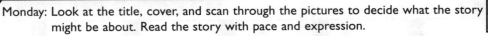

Stage 9   The Litter Queen   Year 2 Term 3

Shared reading and writing

Monday: Look at the title, cover, and scan through the pictures to decide what the story might be about. Read the story with pace and expression.

Tuesday: Reread the story using the discussion pointers from *Teacher's Guide 3* page 155. Find the answers to questions about the story in the text.

Wednesday: Read the story. Use the other general discussion ideas about the story from page 156 *Teacher's Guide 3* to recall events and reasons for them.

Thursday: Read from page 20 to the end again. Use remaining general discussion points from page 156 *Teacher's Guide 3* to talk about litter, picnics, and nightmares.

Friday: Shared writing: Read children's story plans written this week to discuss and reinforce good ideas and good planning notes.

Word work

Revise syllables in words; the need for grammatical agreement, matching verbs to nouns and pronouns.

Monday: Think of and list words ending in *ear*. Separate the list into words that rhyme, e.g. *bear*, *pear*; *hear*, *fear*.

Tuesday: List words ending with *ush*. Sort into lists of words that rhyme with *rush* and those that rhyme with *push*.

Wednesday: Collect *ough* and *ought* words. Practise spelling these words.

Thursday: Make up sentences using full stops, exclamation marks, or question marks at the end.

Friday: Practise spelling or reading high frequency words or spelling patterns learned this week.

Guided group tasks (reading or writing)

Reading: Introduce the story. Scan the text for new words, such as micro-light. Use the picture then syllables and phonemes to read it. Read independently. Ask the children what they found out about the Litter Queen. What kind of a person was she?

Writing: Ask the children to work in pairs to find and write parts of the text that show the character of the Litter Queen, e.g. page 21, 'she shouted crossly', 'he was afraid of the Litter Queen.'

Independent activities

1: Read familiar books or use Magpies Stage 9 workbooks.

Group Activity Sheets Book 3: To use the notes on page 111 to introduce the following:

2: Word work (page 112) to reinforce work on discriminating syllables.

3: Sentence work (page 113) as to the need for grammatical agreement, matching verbs to nouns or pronouns.

4: Text work (page 114) to write sustained stories, using their knowledge of story elements, characterisation, dialogue, and the language of story.

5: 'Don't be a litterbug' poster on Activity Sheet 12 *Teacher's Guide 3*.

Plenary

Use this time to allow children to explain their work to others. It is also an opportunity to reinforce teaching points as they arise and to add to the morning's word work.

Suggested Weekly Plan — THE LITTER QUEEN — STAGE 9 — YEAR 2 TERM 3

Day	Whole class – shared reading and writing.	Whole class – phonics, spelling, vocabulary, grammar.	Guided group tasks (reading or writing)	Guided group tasks (reading or writing)	Independent group tasks			Plenary
Mon	Predict story from title and cover. Read the story.	Clap syllables in words from the text. Use phonemes to spell words one syllable at a time.	**Group A** Guided reading. Syllables, GAS Bk3 p112. — T	**Group B** Workbook or read familiar book. Guided reading or writing. — T	**Group C** Agreement in sentences, GAS Bk3 p113. — I	**Group D** 'Don't be a litter-bug' poster, TG3 Magpies AS12. — I	**Group E** Plan a story, GAS Bk3 p114. — OA	**Group A** Explain syllables puzzle.
Tues	Use discussion pointers, TG3 p155. Use text to check answers to questions.	Find words in text with given number of syllables. Spell the words.	**Group E** As above — T	**Group A** As above — T	**Group B** As above — I	**Group C** As above — I	**Group D** As above — OA	**Group D** Read story plans.
Wed	Use general discussion, TG3 p156 ('The story'), to recall incidents and reasons for them.	Pronouns. Make up sentences with *I, my; he, his; she, her; we, our, you, your; they, their.*	**Group D** As above — T	**Group E** As above — T	**Group A** As above — I	**Group B** As above — I	**Group C** As above — OA	**Group C** Read story plans.
Thur	Use remaining general discussion questions, TG3 p156, to generate wider discussion.	Make up sentences using a name or names with *his, her, their.*	**Group C** As above — T	**Group D** As above — T	**Group E** As above — I	**Group A** As above — I	**Group B** As above — OA	**Group E** Read sentences.
Fri	Use children's story plans, GAS Bk3 p114, to reinforce good ideas and notes for planning a story.	Practise/revise this week's high frequency words or spelling patterns.	**Group B** As above — T	**Group C** As above — T	**Group D** As above — I	**Group E** As above — I	**Group A** As above — OA	**Group B** Explain how syllables work.

Fitting in with the National Literacy Framework

Word work: W2 to reinforce work on discriminating syllables in reading and spelling; W1 to secure phonemic spellings from previous five terms.

Sentence work: S2 the need for grammatical agreement, matching verbs to nouns and pronouns; using simple gender forms correctly.

Text work: T10 to write sustained stories, using knowledge of story elements.

T = Teacher   I = Independent   OA = Other adult

These weekly plans are intended as exemplars only and teachers will want to exercise their own skill and judgement when planning for the Literacy Hour.

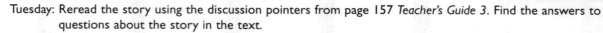

Stage 9   The Quest   Year 2 Term 3

Shared reading and writing

Monday: Look at the title, cover, and scan through the pictures to decide what the story might be about. Read the story with pace and expression.

Tuesday: Reread the story using the discussion pointers from page 157 *Teacher's Guide 3*. Find the answers to questions about the story in the text.

Wednesday: Read the story. Use the other general discussion ideas about the story from page 158 *Teacher's Guide 3*.

Thursday: Read from page 16 to the end. Use remaining general discussion points on page 158 *Teacher's Guide 3* to talk about writing stories, mythical creatures and quests.

Friday: Shared writing: Read children's story plans written this week to discuss and reinforce good ideas and good planning notes.

Word work

Practise and secure phonemic spelling; revise commas in lists; practise sight recognition of Stage 9 words.

Monday: Remind the children how to break the word down into syllables and phonemes for spelling. Words to practise could include: *quest, dentist, forest, rocky, desert, toast*.

Tuesday: Choose more words from the story and practise using phonemes to spell them, e.g. *frightened, kitchen, expecting, tomorrow, cracked, angrily, remember*.

Wednesday: Remind the children how to use commas when writing lists in sentences, e.g. 'Four magic key stories are ...'.

Thursday: Practise sight recognition of Stage 9 words using page 127 *Group Activity Sheets Book 3*.

Friday: Practise spelling or reading high frequency words or spelling patterns learned this week.

Guided group tasks (reading or writing)

Reading: Introduce the story. Ask the children to scan the text for words they do not recognize (e.g. *basilisk*). Segment into phonemes to read the word and use the context and pictures to make sense of it. Read independently. Ask the children what they thought of Wilma's story.

Writing: Ask the children to write a short description of a 'basilisk' so that other children will know what it is. Use the pictures and story and discuss the best words.

Independent activities

1: Read familiar books or use Magpies Stage 9 workbooks.

Group Activity Sheets Book 3: Use the notes on page 115 to introduce the following:

2: Word work (page 116) to secure phonemic spelling.

3: Sentence work (page 117) to use commas in lists.

4: Text work (page 118) to write sustained stories, using their knowledge of story elements, characterization, dialogue, and the language of story.

5: If another adult is available use pages 124 and 125 to assess spelling of high frequency words from Appendix List 1. For independent work use 'Look it up' Activity Sheet 15 from *Teacher's Guide 3*, finishing sentences by referring to the text.

Plenary

Use this time to allow children to explain their work to others. It is also an opportunity to reinforce teaching points as they arise and to add to the morning's word work.

Suggested Weekly Plan — THE QUEST — STAGE 9 — YEAR 2 TERM 3

Day	Whole class – shared reading and writing.	Whole class – phonics, spelling, vocabulary, grammar.	Guided group tasks (reading or writing)	Guided group tasks (reading or writing)	Independent group tasks	Independent group tasks	Independent group tasks	Plenary
Mon	Predict story from title and cover. Read the story.	Choose words from the text to spell using syllables and phonemes, e.g. rocky desert.	**Group A** Guided reading. Spelling, GAS Bk3 p116. — T	**Group B** Workbook or read familiar book. Guided reading or writing. — T	**Group C** Commas in lists, GAS Bk3 p17. — I	**Group D** Planning a story, 'The Quest', GAS Bk3 p118. Begin story writing. — I	**Group E** Assess spelling of Appendix List I, GAS Bk3 p124,125. — OA	**Group C** Read and explain commas in lists work.
Tues	Use discussion pointers, TG3 p157. Use text to check answers to questions.	Choose more words to revise phonemic knowledge, e.g. frightened, angrily.	**Group E** As above — T	**Group A** As above — T	**Group B** As above — I	**Group C** As above — I	**Group D** As above — OA	**Group E** Read work and check spellings.
Wed	Use general discussion ideas, TG3 p158 ('The story'), to discuss events and reasons for them.	Revise use of commas in lists, e.g. 'Four magic key stories are ...'.	**Group D** As above — T	**Group E** As above — T	**Group A** As above — I	**Group B** As above — I	**Group C** As above — OA	**Group B** Read story plans.
Thur	Use remaining discussion ideas, TG3 p158, to generate wider discussion.	Practise sight recognition of Stage 9 words, GAS Bk3 p127.	**Group C** As above — T	**Group D** As above — T	**Group E** As above — I	**Group A** As above — I	**Group B** As above — OA	**Group A** Read story plans
Fri	Review and reinforce children's best ideas for 'The Quest' story plan.	Practise/revise this week's high frequency words or spelling patterns.	**Group B** As above — T	**Group C** As above — T	**Group D** As above — I	**Group E** As above — I	**Group A** As above — OA	**Group D** Read lists with commas.

Fitting in with the National Literacy Framework

Word work: W1 to secure phonemic spelling from previous five terms; **W4** to secure reading and spelling of all the high frequency words from Appendix List 1; **W5** to read on sight high frequency words likely to occur in graded texts matched to the ability of reading groups.

Sentence work: S4 to use commas in lists.

Text work: T10 to write sustained stories, using their knowledge of story elements.

T = Teacher   I = Independent   OA = Other adult

These weekly plans are intended as exemplars only and teachers will want to exercise their own skill and judgement when planning for the Literacy Hour.

Stage 9   Survival Adventure   Year 2 Term 3

Shared reading and writing

Monday: Look at the title, cover, and scan through the pictures to decide what the story might be about. Read the story with pace and expression.

Tuesday: Reread the story using the discussion pointers from *Teacher's Guide 3* page 159. Find the answers to questions about the story in the text.

Wednesday: Read the story. Use the other general discussion ideas about the story from page 160 *Teacher's Guide 3*.

Thursday: Read from page 20 to the end. Use general discussion points on page 160 *Teacher's Guide 3* to talk about wagon trains, Native Americans, and survival kits.

Friday: Shared writing: Read children's story plans written this week to discuss and reinforce good ideas and good planning notes.

Word work

Revise and secure phonemic spellings: *or*, *au*, *aw*, *oor*, and long vowel phonemes.

Monday: Revise words with *or* phonemes and list according to spelling pattern. You could start with *torch*, *jaws*, *caught*, *door*, and *store*.

Tuesday: Add more words to the *or* phonemes lists and practise spelling them.

Wednesday: Revise and spell words with the long vowel phonemes *ai* and *ee*.

Thursday: Revise and spell words with the long vowel phonemes *ie*, *oa*, *ue*.

Friday: Practise spelling or reading high frequency words or spelling patterns learned this week.

Guided group tasks (reading or writing)

Reading: Introduce the story. Talk about the setting, time, and place. Read the story independently. Ask the children to tell you which parts of the story are based on facts. Which parts are fiction?

Writing: Discuss fact and fiction. Ask the children to use the book to write sentences-that are facts, e.g. 'Bears can be dangerous.'

Independent activities

1: Read familiar books or use Magpies Stage 9 workbooks.

Group Activity Sheets Book 3: Use the notes on page 119 to introduce the following:

2: Word work (page 120) to secure phonemic spelling.

3: Sentence work (page 121) to show the need for grammatical agreement using simple gender forms correctly.

4: Text work (page 122) to understand the distinction between fact and fiction; to use the terms *fact* and *fiction* appropriately.

5: If another adult is available, use pages 124 and 125 to continue to assess spelling of high frequency words from Appendix List 1. For independent work use 'What do you know?' Activity Sheet 20 from *Teacher's Guide 3*. Write sentences about Amy.

Plenary

Use this time to allow children to explain their work to others. It is also an opportunity to reinforce teaching points as they arise and to add to the morning's word work.

Suggested Weekly Plan — SURVIVAL ADVENTURE — STAGE 9 — YEAR 2 TERM 3

	Whole class – shared reading and writing.	Whole class – phonics, spelling, vocabulary, grammar.	Guided group tasks (reading or writing)	Guided group tasks (reading or writing)	Independent group tasks			Plenary
Mon	Predict story from title and cover. Read the story together with pace and expression.	Revise *or*, *au*, *aw*, and *oor* words. Make lists. Practise spelling them.	**Group A** Guided reading. An *or* wordsearch, GAS Bk3 p120. **T**	**Group B** Workbook or read familiar book. Assess recognition of Stage 9 words. **T**	**Group C** Pronouns in sentences, GAS Bk3 p121. **I**	**Group D** Fact or fiction? GAS Bk3 p122. **I**	**Group E** Continue to assess spelling of Appendix List I, GAS Bk3 pp124, 125. **OA**	**Group C** Read sentences. Check that pronouns agree.
Tues	Use discussion pointers, TG3 p159. Use text to check answers to questions.	Add more words to *or* phoneme lists and practise spelling them.	**Group E** As above **T**	**Group A** As above **T**	**Group B** As above **I**	**Group C** As above **I**	**Group D** As above **OA**	**Group E** Explain wordsearch.
Wed	Use general discussion, TG3 p160 ('The story'), to discuss events and reasons.	Spell words with long vowel phonemes *ai*, *ee*.	**Group D** As above **T**	**Group E** As above **T**	**Group A** As above **I**	**Group B** As above **I**	**Group C** As above **OA**	**Group B** Explain fact or fiction work.
Thur	Use remaining general discussion ideas, TG3 p160, to generate wider discussion.	Spell words with long vowel phonemes *ie*, *oa*, *ue*.	**Group C** As above **T**	**Group D** As above **T**	**Group E** As above **I**	**Group A** As above **I**	**Group B** As above **OA**	**Group A** Explain fact or fiction work.
Fri	Use index in reference books to find facts about Native Americans. Teacher scribes.	Practise/revise this week's high frequency words or spelling patterns.	**Group B** As above **T**	**Group C** As above **T**	**Group D** As above **I**	**Group E** As above **I**	**Group A** As above **OA**	**Group D** Read pronouns in sentences. Check for agreement.

Fitting in with the National Literacy Framework

Word work: W1 to secure phonemic spelling from previous five terms (*or*, *au*, *aw*, *oor*, and long vowel phonemes).

Sentence work: S2 the need for grammatical agreement, using simple gender forms correctly.

Text work: T13 to understand the distinction between fact and fiction and to use the terms *fact* and *fiction* appropriately; **T15** to use a contents page and index to find way about text.

T = Teacher   **I = Independent**   **OA = Other adult**

These weekly plans are intended as exemplars only and teachers will want to exercise their own skill and judgement when planning for the Literacy Hour.